Weigh to Win *Weight Management System*

THE
WEIGH
TO WIN
COOK
BOOK

LYNN HILL
FOUNDER OF WEIGH TO WIN, INC.

VICTOR BOOKS

A DIVISION OF SCRIPTURE PRESS PUBLICATIONS INC.
USA CANADA ENGLAND

Cover Designer: Scott Rattray
Cover Photo: The Image Bank

2 3 4 5 6 7 8 9 10 Printing/Year 96 95 94 93 92

TABLE OF CONTENTS

Letter from Lynn Hill 5

Explanatory Notes 6

Basic Measurements 9

Metric Conversions 9

Abbreviations 9

Breads and Starches 11

Eggs 21

Fish 31

Fruits 37

Meat and Poultry 47

Milk 55

Vegetables, Salads, and Sauces 65

Liver 79

Index 83

A LETTER FROM LYNN HILL

Are you tired of dietetic recipe books that require strange ingredients or take hours to prepare? You will be happy to know the recipes contained in *The Weigh to Win Cookbook* use ingredients you most generally have on hand and are quick and easy to prepare.

The recipes are what I call TTT's (tried, tested, and true) because they have been submitted by our *Weigh to Win* members and approved by our registered dietitian, Marla Smith. Many of the recipes contained in the book are those which have quickly become *Weigh to Win* favorites such as our Unbelievable Lasagna and Oat Bran Muffins.

You will find recipes for quick breakfasts for those who "don't have time to eat," convenient main dishes, lovely desserts, and handy snacks.

All this adds up to making your healthy weight loss rewarding and easy. That is what *Weigh to Win* has always been about —helping you lose weight in a safe, simple, and sensible way.

What our members have discovered is that eating nutritiously can be tasty, interesting, easy, and a lot of fun!

If you are not a member of *Weigh to Win*, we would encourage you to call our toll-free number for information on the *Weigh to Win Weight Management System*.

Weigh to Win uses no pills, no supplements, and no special foods. We teach you the skills you need to make healthy food choices whether shopping, eating out, or having a delicious meal at home.

The *Weigh to Win* approach is that most people overeat for reasons other than rebellion to God's laws. Overeating due to emotional problems (stress, loneliness, depression, painful memories) or eating foods high in calories and fat because, "That's the way Mom cooked!" is not a sin problem. It is simply learned behavior which needs to be evaluated and changed with God's help. God looks at the heart and does not judge us by how much we weigh.

Weigh to Win is not affiliated with any church but provides help and encouragement for people of all faiths to be able to succeed at losing weight. Members have expressed an appreciation for this positive perspective of the *Weigh to Win Weight Management System*.

Weigh to Win weight-loss resources both for individuals and support groups are available at most Christian bookstores. For more information, call or write:

Weigh to Win, Inc.

113 E. Washington
Suite 108
Plymouth, Indiana 46563

1-800-642-THIN(8446) or 219-935-5191

Now, blessings to you as you use these delicious recipes to achieve your dreams of a healthier, trimmer you!

"So whether you eat or drink or whatever you do, do it all for the glory of God" (1 Corinthians 10:31, NIV).

God bless you,

Lynn Hill

Founder and President
Weigh to Win, Inc.

EXPLANATORY NOTES

This cookbook may be enjoyed by anyone concerned with preparing low fat, low sugar, and low calorie meals. However, the exchange amounts listed are designed to be used in conjunction with the *Weigh to Win Weight Management System* only.

Instant nonfat drymilk is to be used *dry* or in *powder* form when called for in recipes in this cookbook. Instant nonfat dry milk may be reconstituted according to package directions and substituted for any recipe calling for *skim milk*.

Diet or reduced calorie mayonnaise is any mayonnaise with 1/2 the amount of calories as the original product.

Nonfat or fat free mayonnaise may be used in any recipe . The number of calories shown on the label for the amount used would count as *Freedom to Choose* calories—NOT as a Fat Exchange.

In recipes calling for *baking powder* or *baking soda,* check the date on the package to ensure freshness or your baking results may be less than satisfactory.

Artificial sweeteners have always been optional with *Weigh to Win.* Sugar or honey may be substituted in any recipe calling for artificial sweeteners by using *Freedom to Choose* calories (1/2 tsp. of sugar or honey = 10 FTC calories).

Equal or *Nutrasweet* may NOT be used for baking or in recipes which require heating for a prolonged period of time. Unless the recipe specifically calls for Equal, use another artificial sweetener such as Sweet N Low which does not break down with prolonged heating.

Some recipes call for NONfat yogurt and others call for LOWfat yogurt. Be sure to note which yogurt is required as each counts differently on the *Weigh to Win* Rainbow Food Plan.

For healthy weight loss DO NOT eat or drink the following except for approved recipes in this book:

- alcoholic beverages
- butter
- cake, candy, cookies
- doughnuts
- fried foods
- frozen yogurt, ices
- gravy
- ice cream
- muffins
- nuts, chips, pretzels
- pancakes, waffles
- pies, puddings
- soft drinks (except sugar free)
- yogurt (except plain or dietetic)

Weigh and measure your portions with a diet scale and standard measuring cups and spoons. Divide portions evenly if more than one serving is prepared.

If it is noted that *diet bread* is NOT to be used, it is generally because diet bread will not achieve the same results as regular bread in the recipe.

Limited Vegetables are tomato juice, tomato sauce, tomato puree, and tomato paste. Note if these foods are called for in the recipe which you are preparing and use only in the amounts allowed on the *Weigh to Win* Rainbow Food Plan.

Limited Proteins are as follows:

Eggs ....Limited to 4 exchanges
                             per week
Beef, Lamb & Pork ...Limited to 10 exchanges
                             per week
Cheese ....Limited to 4 exchanges
                             per week
Liver ....Limited to 6 exchanges
                             per week

Recipes containing any of these foods are not only counted as Protein Exchanges on the "Daily Exchanges" section of the Weekly Food Record but *also* must be accounted for by *Weigh to Win* members under the section "Weekly Exchanges" on the Weekly Food Record. Always note if any of these Limited Protein foods are listed in the ingredients of the recipe and account for them according to the allowed amounts of the *Weigh to Win* Rainbow Food Plan.

KEY TO SYMBOLS
The shaded box at the end of each recipe in this cookbook provides single-serving information and correlates to the six food-group exchanges in the *Weigh to Win Weight Management System* Rainbow Food Plan. The circle symbols quickly communicate the number of exchanges per recipe and allow you to easily tabulate your daily/weekly allowances on the system's Weekly Food Record sheets. Freedom to Choose calories are listed numerically, where applicable.

● = 1 exchange   ◖ = 3/4 exchange
◗ = 1/2 exchange   ◞ = 1/4 exchange

BASIC MEASUREMENTS

Volume Measures

Pinch = about 1/16 teaspoon
Dash = 6 drops or about 1/8 teaspoon
3 teaspoons = 1 tablespoon
2 tablespoons = 1/8 cup or 1 fluid ounce
4 tablespoons = 1/4 cup or 2 fluid ounces
5 1/3 tablespoons = 1/3 cup
8 tablespoons = 1/2 cup or 4 fluid ounces
10 2/3 tablespoons = 2/3 cup
12 tablespoons = 3/4 cup or 6 fluid ounces
16 tablespoons = 1 cup or 1/2 pint or 8 fluid ounces
1 pint = 2 cups or 16 fluid ounces
2 pint s = 4 cups or 1 quart or 32 fluid ounces
1 liter = 1 quart plus 3 fluid ounces

Weights

2 ounces   = 1/8 pound
4 ounces   = 1/4 pound
8 ounces   = 1/2 pound
16 ounces   = 1 pound

Abbreviations

tsp. or t.   = teaspoon
Tbsp. or T.   = tablespoon
c.   = cup
lb.   = pound
oz.   = ounce
pkg.   = package
pkt.   = packet
lg.   = large
sm.   = small
FTC   = Freedom to Choose

Weights of Meat

Raw		Cooked
8 ounces	=	6 ounces
6 ounces	=	4 ounces
4 ounces	=	3 ounces
3 ounces	=	2 ounces

Metric Conversions

Dry or Liquid Measure
1 tsp.   = 5 milliliters
1 Tbsp. = 15 milliliters
16 Tbsp. = 1 cup = .24 liter

Liquid Measure
1 oz.   = 2 Tbsp. = 30 milliliters
1 cup   = 8 fl. oz. = .24 liter (240 ml)
2 cups = 1 pint   = .47 liter (470 ml)
4 cups = 1 quart = .95 liter (950 ml)

Weight
1 oz.   = 28 grams
1 pound = 16 oz. = .45 kilograms (454 grams)

Cooking time per pound x 2.2 = cooking time per kilogram

Approximate temperature conversions from Fahrenheit to Centigrade:

Fahrenheit	Centigrade
450	230
425	220
400	200
375	190
350	180
325	170
300	150

BREADS

BAKED SQUASH

Each 1/2 cup = 1 serving.

1 medium acorn squash

Cut squash in half. Remove seeds. Place cut side down on a baking sheet coated with nonstick cooking spray. Bake at 400 degrees 45-60 minutes or until tender.

2 tsp. Sugar Twin brown sugar substitute
1 tsp. water

Turn right side up; sprinkle with Sugar Twin and water. Continue to bake right side up about 15 minutes longer.

One serving counts as:	Fruit	Milk	Bread ●
Freedom to Choose Calories:	Vegetable	Fat	Protein

ALMOST A PIE

Makes 4 servings.

2 c. skim milk
4 large eggs
1 1/2 tsp. vanilla extract
1/2 tsp. coconut extract
6 Tbsp. flour
2 slices bread (not diet), torn in pieces
dash of salt
Sweet N Low to equal one-half cup sugar (12 pkts.)

Mix at high speed in blender. Pour in large pie pan coated with nonstick cooking spray. Bake at 350 degrees for 45-50 minutes.

VARIATIONS:
CHOCOLATE—Add 4 tsp. cocoa. (*Add 5 Freedom to Choose Calories to each serving.*)
COCONUT— Add 4 tsp. unsweetened coconut and 1 tsp. coconut flavoring. (*Add 10 Freedom to Choose Calories to each serving.*)

One serving counts as:	Fruit	Milk ◖	Bread ●
Freedom to Choose Calories:	Vegetable	Fat	Protein ●

FRUIT DANISH DELIGHT

Makes 1 serving.

1/2 small apple, peeled, cored, and grated
1/4 c. part skim ricotta cheese
1 pkt. Sweet N Low
1/4 tsp. cinnamon
1 slice crisp toast, whole wheat or white (not diet)

Combine first four ingredients. Pile on toast and broil until heated through and slightly browned on top.

One serving counts as:	Fruit ●	Milk	Bread ●
Freedom to Choose Calories:	Vegetable	Fat	Protein ●

PUMPKIN PUDDING

Makes 2 servings.

1 envelope (1 Tbsp.) unflavored gelatin
1/4 c. cold water

Soften gelatin in cold water.

1/4 c. boiling water
1 c. pumpkin
1 tsp. vanilla extract
2 pkts. Equal
2/3 c. instant nonfat dry milk
4 ice cubes
1/4 tsp. pumpkin pie spice

Add rest of ingredients and mix in blender.

One serving counts as:	Fruit	Milk ●	Bread ●
Freedom to Choose Calories:	Vegetable	Fat	Protein

PLEASING PUMPKIN PIE

Makes 4 servings.

No eggs—No cholesterol!

2 c. canned pumpkin
1/4 c. Sugar Twin, brown sugar replacement
1/4 tsp. rum extract
1/8 tsp. nutmeg
1/8 tsp. cinnamon
1/8 tsp. ginger

Combine first 6 ingredients in large bowl; mix well. Set aside.

2 envelopes (2 Tbsp.) unflavored gelatin
1/4 c. cold water

Sprinkle gelatin over water in small saucepan to soften. Place over low heat and stir until gelatin has dissolved, about 3 minutes. Set aside.

1 c. evaporated skimmed milk
2 pkts. Sweet N Low

Combine milk and Sweet N Low in bowl; mix with electric mixer. Slowly pour in gelatin mixture and continue beating until stiff peaks form. Fold 3/4 of this mixture into pumpkin mixture. Pour into 8" pie pan coated with nonstick cooking spray. Top with remaining gelatin mixture. Chill until firm.

One serving counts as:	Fruit	Milk ◖	Bread ●
Freedom to Choose Calories:	Vegetable	Fat	Protein

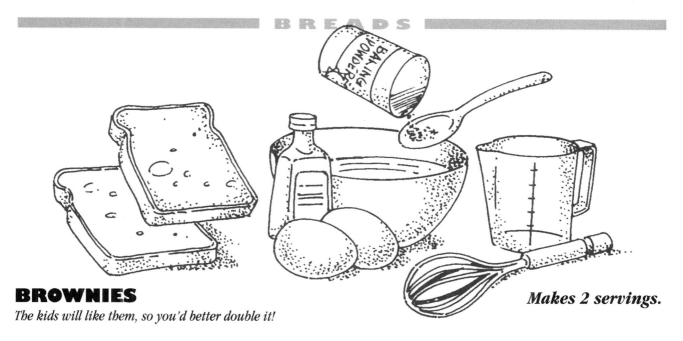

BROWNIES

Makes 2 servings.

The kids will like them, so you'd better double it!

2 large eggs, separated
1/4 c. water

In bowl beat egg yolks with water.

2 slices bread (not diet), crumbed
2 pkts. sugar-free chocolate shake mix
1/2 tsp. baking powder
1/4 tsp. maple extract
1 pkt. Sweet N Low

Add bread crumbs, shake mix, baking powder, extract, and Sweet N Low; mix well.

Beat egg whites until stiff but not dry. Fold into chocolate mixture. Pour into 8" square pan coated with nonstick cooking spray. Bake at 350 degrees for 10-12 minutes or until it tests done. Cool.

One serving counts as:	Fruit	Milk ●	Bread ●
Freedom to Choose Calories:	Vegetable	Fat	Protein ●

MACARONI CHEESE BAKE

Makes 2 servings.

1/2 c. evaporated skimmed milk
1/3 c. instant nonfat dry milk

Combine evaporated milk and dry milk; heat over low heat.

salt and pepper to taste
2 Tbsp. diet margarine
1 c. cooked macaroni
2 oz. shredded cheddar cheese

Add remaining ingredients. Bake for 30 minutes at 350 degrees in a casserole dish coated with nonstick cooking spray.

One serving counts as:	Fruit	Milk ●	Bread ●
Freedom to Choose Calories:	Vegetable	Fat ●◖	Protein ●

WHOLE WHEAT MUFFINS

Makes 2 servings.

2 slices whole wheat bread (not diet), crumbed
2/3 c. instant nonfat dry milk
4 pkts. Sweet N Low
2 tsp. baking powder

Mix dry ingredients.

2 Tbsp. diet margarine
2 large eggs, beaten

Stir in eggs and margarine.

1/2 c. blueberries OR 1 small banana,
    mashed OR 1 small apple, chopped

Fold in fruit.

Divide evenly into a six-cup muffin tin sprayed with nonstick cooking spray. Bake 25 minutes at 375 degrees.

One serving counts as:	Fruit ◖	Milk ●	Bread ●
Freedom to Choose Calories:	Vegetable	Fat ●◖	Protein ●

RHUBARB PIE

Makes 4 servings.

4 large eggs

Beat eggs until fluffy.

4 slices unbuttered toast (not diet),
    crumbed
1 tsp. baking soda
1 1/3 c. instant nonfat dry milk
1 Tbsp. & 1 tsp. oil
1 c. water
4 c. rhubarb
1/2 - 2/3 c. Sugar Twin
1/4 tsp. nutmeg or cinnamon

Mix remaining ingredients in another bowl. Add eggs, then pour into an 8" x 8" baking pan coated with nonstick cooking spray.

Bake at 350 degrees for 45 minutes.

One serving counts as:	Fruit	Milk ●	Bread ●
Freedom to Choose Calories:	Vegetable ●●	Fat ●	Protein ●

APPLE SPICED OATMEAL

Makes 1 serving.

1 oz. uncooked oatmeal
1/2 small apple, cored, peeled, and sliced very thin
1/4 tsp. cinnamon
1/4 tsp. nutmeg
1 tsp. orange extract
1 tsp. diet margarine
Sweet N Low brown sugar replacement to taste (opt.)
1/2 c. skim milk

Cook cereal according to package directions, except add apple to water before cooking. Stir in rest of ingredients and serve hot.

One serving counts as:	Fruit ◖	Milk ◖	Bread ●
Freedom to Choose Calories:	Vegetable	Fat ◖	Protein

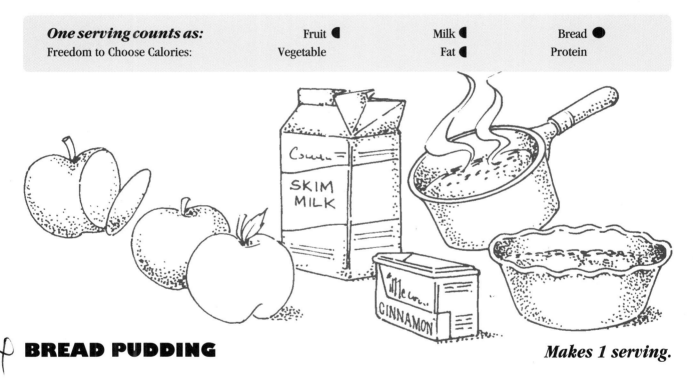

BREAD PUDDING

Makes 1 serving.

1 c. skim milk
1 large egg, beaten
1 tsp. vanilla extract
1 pkt. Sweet N Low

1 slice bread (not diet)

VARIATION: Add 2 Tbsp. raisins and 1 tsp. cinnamon.
(Add 1 Fruit Exchange.)

Heat milk; add egg, vanilla, and Sweet N Low.

Pour over bread in small casserole dish coated with nonstick cooking spray. Set dish in pan of water and bake 45 minutes at 325 degrees.

One serving counts as:	Fruit	Milk ●	Bread ●
Freedom to Choose Calories:	Vegetable	Fat	Protein ●

✝ PUMPKIN DESSERT

Makes 1 serving.

1 large egg, separated
1/2 c. pumpkin
1/4 c. skim milk
1/2 tsp. pumpkin pie spice
2 pkts. Sweet N Low
1/4 tsp. salt

Beat egg yolk. Add all ingredients except egg white.

Beat egg white until stiff peaks form; fold into pumpkin mixture. Bake in small casserole coated with nonstick cooking spray for 30 minutes at 350 degrees.

One serving counts as:	Fruit	Milk ◖	Bread ●
Freedom to Choose Calories:	Vegetable	Fat	Protein ●

BREAKFAST BAR

Makes 1 serving.

1/3 c. instant nonfat dry milk
2 tsp. diet margarine
2 tsp. unsweetened cocoa
2 pkts. Equal

Mix dry milk, margarine, cocoa, and Equal well with fork.

1 Tbsp. water
1 oz. crushed cereal
3/4 oz. dried apple

Add remaining ingredients and mix well. Form into squares and freeze 15 minutes.

One serving counts as:	Fruit ●	Milk ●	Bread ●
Freedom to Choose Calories: 10	Vegetable	Fat ●	Protein

MASHED POTATO SURPRISE

Makes 1 serving.

3 oz. cooked pared potato
1 c. cooked pared rutabaga
1/4 c. evaporated skimmed milk
1 tsp. diet margarine
salt and pepper

In medium saucepan, mash potato and rutabaga together with remaining ingredients. Serve hot.

One serving counts as:	Fruit	Milk ◖	Bread ●
Freedom to Choose Calories:	Vegetable ●●	Fat ◖	Protein

OAT BRAN MUFFINS

Makes 1 serving.

1 oz. oat bran cereal
   (available in hot cereal section of store)
1 large egg
1/3 c. instant nonfat dry milk
1 tsp. vanilla extract
1 tsp. baking powder
1 pkt. Sweet N Low
1/4 c. water
2 Tbsp. currants OR raisins
cinnamon and nutmeg to taste

Mix together all ingredients well.

Coat a six-cup muffin tin with nonstick cooking spray and divide mixture evenly in the six cups.

Bake at 350 degrees for about 20 minutes or until just golden on top.

VARIATION: Reduce or eliminate water and add 1 small banana, 1/2 c. blueberries, or 1/2 c. pineapple in place of currants or raisins.

One serving counts as:	Fruit ●	Milk ●	Bread ●
Freedom to Choose Calories:	Vegetable	Fat	Protein ●

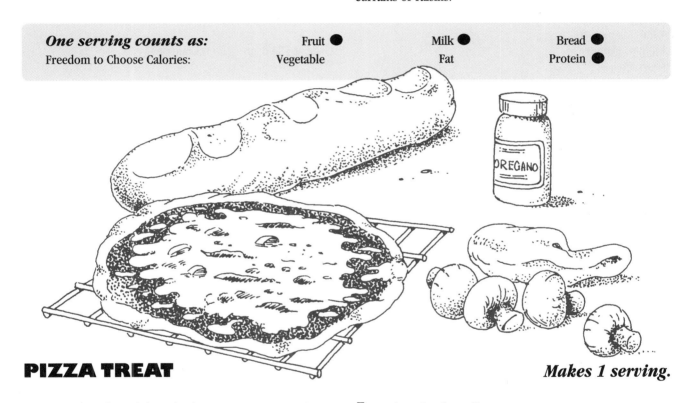

PIZZA TREAT

Makes 1 serving.

1 slice Italian bread (not diet)

2 Tbsp. tomato sauce
1/8 tsp. oregano
dash garlic powder

1 Tbsp. diced green pepper
1 Tbsp. sliced mushrooms
2 oz. mozzarella cheese

Flatten bread with a rolling pin.

Mix oregano and garlic powder with tomato sauce; spread on flattened bread.

Top with green pepper, mushrooms, and cheese. Bake at 400 degrees for 10-15 minutes.

One serving counts as:	Fruit	Milk	Bread ●
Freedom to Choose Calories:	Vegetable ◖	Fat	Protein ●●

GINGERBREAD

Makes 4 servings.

4 slices bread (not diet), crumbed
4 small apples, diced
4 large eggs, separated

1 1/3 c. instant nonfat dry milk
Brown sugar substitute to equal 2 Tbsp. & 2 tsp.
    brown sugar
1/4 c. water
4 tsp. cinnamon
1 Tbsp. ginger
1 tsp. cloves
2 tsp. baking soda
1/2 tsp. cream of tartar
1/2 tsp. salt

Mix bread, apple, and egg yolks until smooth.

Add remaining ingredients except egg whites, cream of tartar, and salt. Set mixture aside. Beat egg whites, cream of tartar, and salt until stiff. Fold into apple mixture. Place mixture in a loaf pan lined with waxed paper.

Bake at 350 degrees for 45 minutes.

One serving counts as:	Fruit ●	Milk ●	Bread ●
Freedom to Choose Calories:	Vegetable	Fat	Protein ●

POTATO CHARLIES

Makes 1 serving.

3 oz. cooked potato
1/2 tsp. instant nonfat dry milk
1 tsp. water
2 tsp. diet margarine
1/4 tsp. celery salt
1/2 tsp. dried onion flakes
dash salt and pepper

3 oz. cooked tuna, flaked
paprika

Mash potato with fork; add dry milk, water, margarine, celery salt, dried onion flakes, salt, and pepper. Mix well.

Add tuna and shape into 1 1/2" diameter balls. Sprinkle with paprika. Place on nonstick baking sheet.

Bake at 350 degrees for 25 minutes.

One serving counts as:	Fruit	Milk	Bread ●
Freedom to Choose Calories: 3	Vegetable	Fat ●	Protein ● ● ●

BLUEBERRY PANCAKES

Makes 2 servings.

2 slices bread (not diet), crumbed
2 large eggs
1/2 c. plain low fat yogurt
1/2 tsp. Sweet N Low
2 Tbsp. flour

Blend all ingredients except blueberries in blender.

1 c. blueberries

Then fold in the blueberries. Cook in a skillet coated with nonstick cooking spray.

One serving counts as:	Fruit ●	Milk ◖	Bread ●
Freedom to Choose Calories: **30**	Vegetable	Fat	Protein ●

CHOCOLATE APPLESAUCE CUPCAKES

Makes 2 servings.

1 c. unsweetened applesauce
1 tsp. baking soda
1 tsp. baking powder
dash salt
1/2 tsp. allspice
1 Tbsp. unsweetened cocoa
2 pkts. Sweet N Low
2 pkts. sugar-free chocolate shake mix
2 slices bread (not diet), crumbed
1 tsp. vanilla extract

Combine all ingredients and beat well. Divide mixture into 8 cupcake tins coated with nonstick cooking spray.

Bake at 350 degrees for 25 minutes.

One serving counts as:	Fruit ●	Milk ●	Bread ●
Freedom to Choose Calories: **8**	Vegetable	Fat	Protein

EGGS

FRENCH TOAST

Makes 1 serving.

1 slice bread (not diet)
1 large egg
1/4 c. skim milk
artificial sweetener
cinnamon

Soak the slice of bread in egg and milk. Broil on both sides, then sprinkle with artificial sweetener and cinnamon.

1 small apple

Slice apple and arrange on plate at side of toast in an attractive design.

One serving counts as:	Fruit ●	Milk ◖	Bread ●
Freedom to Choose Calories:	Vegetable	Fat	Protein ●

CINNAMON APPLE BREAD PUDDING

Makes 6 servings.

6 slices cinnamon raisin bread (not diet)

Lightly toast bread and cut into large cubes. Layer half of bread in 8" square baking dish sprayed with nonstick cooking spray.

3 small diced Golden Delicious apples

Spread apples evenly on bread cubes. Top with remaining bread cubes.

2 Tbsp. margarine
1 1/2 c. skim milk

Heat milk and margarine only until margarine melts.

6 large eggs, beaten
2 Tbsp. packed brown sugar *plus*
    brown sugar substitute to equal 1/3 c. sugar
1/2 tsp. grated lemon peel
1/4 tsp. nutmeg
dash salt

Combine eggs, brown sugar, brown sugar substitute, and seasonings; gradually add milk, stirring constantly. Pour mixture over bread and apples.

Bake uncovered at 350 degrees for 40-45 minutes or until set and knife inserted near center comes out clean. Serve warm or cold.

One serving counts as:	Fruit ◖	Milk ◖	Bread ●
Freedom to Choose Calories: **20**	Vegetable	Fat ●	Protein ●

EGG FOO YUNG

Makes 4 servings.

3 c. mushrooms, sliced
2 Tbsp. chicken broth
1/2 c. onion, diced
1 c. celery, diced

Cook mushrooms in chicken broth for 1 minute; add onion and celery. Stir. Saute 5 minutes; cool.

1/2 c. bean sprouts, drained
4 large eggs
1/4 tsp. salt
1/8 tsp. pepper

Add bean sprouts. Beat eggs until light; add salt and pepper. Add to vegetable mixture.

Place 1/4 of mixture in a hot skillet and cook. Repeat 3 more times.

One serving counts as:	Fruit	Milk	Bread
Freedom to Choose Calories: **1**	Vegetable ●●◖	Fat	Protein ●

DEVILED EGGS

Makes 12 servings.

6 hard boiled large eggs, cut in half lengthwise
1/3 c. cottage cheese
2 Tbsp. skim milk
1 tsp. vinegar
1 tsp. prepared mustard
1/4 tsp. salt
dash each pepper and onion powder

Remove yolks from whites and place in blender with remaining ingredients.

Blend at medium speed until mixture is smooth. Stop blender and scrape sides occasionally. Spoon yolk mixture into egg whites; garnish with snipped parsley or paprika.

One serving counts as:	Fruit	Milk	Bread
Freedom to Choose Calories: **5**	Vegetable	Fat	Protein ◖

BANANA FLUFF PUDDING

Makes 2 servings.

2 large eggs, separated

Beat egg yolks slightly.

2 c. skim milk
1 envelope (1 Tbsp.) unflavored gelatin

Add 1 1/2 c. milk. Mix other 1/2 c. milk with gelatin and add to egg yolk mixture.

1/2 tsp. salt

Stir in salt and cook to a boil. Cool completely. Beat egg whites until stiff.

2 pkts. Equal
2 tsp. vanilla extract
1 small banana

Add dash of Equal to egg whites. Beat pudding in blender until fluffy. Stir in remainder of Equal, vanilla, and banana; fold in egg whites.

One serving counts as:	Fruit ◖	Milk ●	Bread
Freedom to Choose Calories:	Vegetable	Fat	Protein ●

ZUCCHINI OMELET

Makes 1 serving.

1 large egg, beaten
1/4 c. skim milk
1 Tbsp. chopped parsley
1/2 tsp. salt
1/8 tsp. garlic powder
1/4 tsp. pepper

Combine egg, milk, parsley, and seasonings.

1/2 c. diced, cooked zucchini

Add zucchini and cook in nonstick pan over moderate heat until center is almost set, about 4 minutes.

1 oz. slice American cheese

Top with cheese.

Transfer to broiler. Broil about 4" from heat for 3 minutes or until cheese melts. Serve at once.

One serving counts as:	Fruit	Milk ◗	Bread
Freedom to Choose Calories:	Vegetable ●	Fat	Protein ●●

BREAKFAST "TACO"

Makes 1 serving.

1/4 c. lettuce, shredded
1 slice whole wheat bread (not diet), toasted
1 hard cooked large egg, sliced

Spoon lettuce on toast. Arrange egg slices on lettuce.

1/8 tsp. salt
dash each pepper and chili powder
1/4 c. tomato juice, room temperature

Sprinkle with salt, pepper, and chili powder. Slowly pour tomato juice over all.

One serving counts as:	Fruit	Milk	Bread ●
Freedom to Choose Calories:	Vegetable ●	Fat	Protein ●

PINEAPPLE UPSIDE-DOWN CUSTARD

Makes 1 serving.

1 large egg, separated
1 tsp. lemon juice
1/4 tsp. almond extract
dash nutmeg

Beat yolk with fork until light and lemon colored. Stir in lemon juice, almond extract, and nutmeg.

2 Tbsp. & 2 tsp. instant nonfat dry milk

Add dry milk and blend until it makes a thick paste. In a small bowl beat egg white until stiff. Fold egg white gently into yolk mixture.

1/2 c. fresh pineapple, diced
dash artificial sweetener (not Equal)

Arrange pineapple on bottom of pie plate and sprinkle with sweetener. Spread egg mixture over pineapple and bake on bottom shelf of oven at 350 degrees for 30 minutes, or until puffed up and brown.

One serving counts as:	Fruit ●	Milk ◖	Bread
Freedom to Choose Calories:	Vegetable	Fat	Protein ●

MUSHROOM ASPARAGUS OMELET

Makes 2 servings.

1 c. asparagus tips
1/2 c. chicken broth

2 large eggs, lightly beaten
1 Tbsp. water
1/2 c. mushrooms, chopped fine
salt and pepper

Heat asparagus in broth.

Combine eggs, water, and mushrooms. Season with salt and pepper; mix well.

Cook over low heat in preheated 6" nonstick skillet. As mixture sets at edge, with fork draw edges toward center so uncooked portions flow to bottom. Keep mixture as level as possible. When eggs are set and surface is still moist, drain asparagus and discard broth. Place asparagus across center of omelet; with a spatula fold omelet over. Roll onto plate.

One serving counts as:	Fruit	Milk	Bread
Freedom to Choose Calories: **10**	Vegetable ●◖	Fat	Protein ●

CHEESE SOUFFLE

Makes 1 serving.

1/2 c. skim milk
1 large egg, separated
1 oz. sharp cheddar cheese, grated

1 slice bread (not diet), crumbed
1/8 tsp. salt
dash pepper

Combine milk, egg yolk, cheese, and bread crumbs in a saucepan.

Season with salt and pepper. Cook over low heat, stirring until mixture is slightly thickened. Cool. Beat egg white with rotary beater until peaks form; fold into first mixture.

Pour into souffle dish. Bake at 375 degrees for 25 minutes.

One serving counts as:	Fruit	Milk ◖	Bread ●
Freedom to Choose Calories:	Vegetable	Fat	Protein ●●

EGGS AU GRATIN

Makes 2 servings.

2 oz. American cheese, diced
2 Tbsp. skim milk
1/2 tsp. dried onion flakes

2 hard cooked large eggs, chopped
1 Tbsp. chopped celery
1/2 tsp. prepared mustard
1/2 tsp. Worcestershire sauce
salt and pepper
2 slices toast (not diet)

In small saucepan, combine cheese, skim milk, and onion flakes. Remove from heat.

Add remaining ingredients (except toast). Serve hot over toast.

One serving counts as:	Fruit	Milk	Bread ●
Freedom to Choose Calories: **13**	Vegetable	Fat	Protein ●●

SNOW EGGS

Makes 2 servings.

(Sometimes called Floating Island)

Custard Sauce:
2 c. skim milk
6 pkts. Sweet N Low
4 large egg yolks
1/2 tsp. vanilla extract

Scald milk over low heat. Beat yolks and sweetener until light.

Stir a few spoonfuls of scalded milk into yolks, then gradually add the yolk mixture to remaining hot milk, stirring constantly. Return pan to low heat and cook, stirring constantly, until mixture coats spoon. Stir vigorously to smooth out lumps. Transfer to serving dish, then chill until set, stirring once or twice to keep skin from forming.

Snow Eggs:
4 large egg whites
12 pkts. Sweet N Low

Half-fill saucepan with water, heat to simmering. Beat egg whites and sweetener until stiff. Using a wet tablespoon, form the meringue into oval shapes the size of eggs. Slip them off the spoon into the simmering water and poach one layer at a time, on both sides, turning them after 2 minutes. Remove from saucepan with slotted spoon, and dry on paper towels. Serve over chilled Custard Sauce.

One serving counts as:	Fruit	Milk ●	Bread
Freedom to Choose Calories:	Vegetable	Fat	Protein ●●

BAKED FRITTATA

Makes 1 serving.

1 c. cooked, chopped green beans, wax beans, or
    snow peas
2 large eggs, separated

salt and pepper
dash garlic powder
1 Tbsp. minced, fresh herbs (chives, parsley, or
    rosemary) OR 1 tsp. dried herbs
1/4 tsp. fresh chopped chives for garnish

Combine beans with beaten egg yolks.

Add seasonings. Beat egg whites until stiff and fold, 1/3 at a time into vegetable mixture.

Pour batter into a heated heavy iron skillet and bake at 350 degrees for 20 minutes. Cut into wedges and serve from skillet with a sprinkling of fresh chives.

One serving counts as:	Fruit	Milk	Bread
Freedom to Choose Calories:	Vegetable ●●	Fat	Protein ●●

EGGS PIPERADE

Makes 2 servings.

2 Tbsp. dried onion flakes
1 c. cut up tomato

1/2 c. diced green pepper

4 large eggs, beaten
salt and pepper
pinch basil

Soak onion flakes in tomato; if tomato is not ripe and succulent, add a tablespoon or two of water.

Combine with green pepper. Soften vegetable mixture by cooking for a few minutes in a hot nonstick pan.

Combine beaten eggs with salt, pepper, and basil. Add egg mixture to vegetable mixture in pan. Scramble.

One serving counts as:	Fruit	Milk	Bread
Freedom to Choose Calories:	Vegetable ●◖	Fat	Protein ●●

POACHED EGGS AND BROCCOLI

Makes 4 servings.

1 c. cooked broccoli florets
2 tsp. salt
2 tsp. pepper
dash nutmeg

Arrange florets in 4 individual ramekins. Season with salt, pepper, and nutmeg.

4 soft set poached large eggs, drained on paper towels
4 slices bread (not diet), made into crumbs
2 c. skim milk
4 slices hard cheese (1 oz. each)

Add poached egg to each one. Top with bread crumbs, pour in milk, and cover with cheese. Bake at 375 degrees until piping hot and cheese is fully melted.

One serving counts as:	Fruit	Milk ◖	Bread ●
Freedom to Choose Calories:	Vegetable ◖	Fat	Protein ●●

CRUSTLESS ASPARAGUS QUICHE

Makes 2 servings.

2 tsp. margarine, divided
1/4 c. chopped green onions

In small skillet, heat 1 tsp. margarine until bubbly and hot; add onions and saute until softened.

1 c. cooked, chopped asparagus
1/2 c. evaporated skimmed milk
2 large eggs, beaten
2 oz. shredded Swiss cheese, divided
1/4 tsp. pepper
dash each salt and red pepper

In medium bowl combine onions with asparagus, milk, eggs, 1 oz. cheese, and seasonings.

Grease 7" pie plate with remaining 1 tsp. margarine and pour in mixture; sprinkle with remaining cheese. Bake at 375 degrees for 35 minutes until knife inserted in center comes out clean.

One serving counts as:	Fruit	Milk ◖	Bread
Freedom to Choose Calories:	Vegetable ●◖	Fat ●	Protein ●●

COCONUT BREAD PUDDING

Makes 1 serving.

1 c. skim milk
1 large egg
3 pkts. Sweet N Low
1/2 tsp. vanilla extract
1 tsp. coconut extract

Combine all ingredients except bread and cinnamon in blender and blend.

1 slice white bread (not diet), cubed
cinnamon to taste

Pour mixture into small baking dish. Place bread cubes on top and press in.

Sprinkle with cinnamon. Set dish in another pan holding 1/2" of water and bake at 350 degrees for 50 minutes or until knife comes out clean when inserted in mixture.

One serving counts as:	Fruit	Milk ●	Bread ●
Freedom to Choose Calories:	Vegetable	Fat	Protein ●

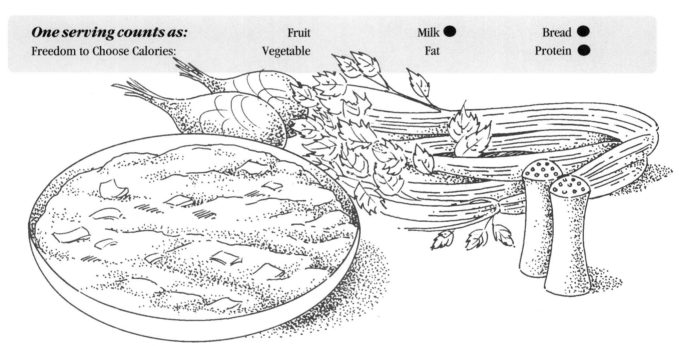

YOGURT EGG SALAD

Makes 2 servings.

2 hard cooked large eggs, chopped
2 Tbsp. plain NONfat yogurt
2 or 3 drops lemon juice
1/2 tsp. prepared mustard
1/2 tsp. vinegar
2 tsp. chopped onion
2 tsp. chopped celery
salt and pepper to taste

Combine all ingredients and fork blend lightly. Serve on lettuce or in sandwiches.

Note: *If used in a sandwich, count the Bread Exchange.*

One serving counts as:	Fruit	Milk	Bread
Freedom to Choose Calories: 6	Vegetable	Fat	Protein ●

FISH

NEW ENGLAND FISH CHOWDER

Makes 1 serving.

3 oz. raw potato, diced
1/2 c. diced onion
6 oz. frozen cod fish fillet

In saucepan combine potato, onion, and fish.

water
salt and pepper to taste

Cover with water and bring to a boil. Add salt and pepper; simmer until vegetables are tender and fish flakes, about 30 minutes.

1/3 c. instant nonfat dry milk
1 tsp. margarine

Add dry milk and stir well. Remove from heat and break fish into bite-size pieces. Add margarine and stir until it melts.

One serving counts as:	Fruit	Milk ●	Bread ●
Freedom to Choose Calories:	Vegetable ●	Fat ●	Protein ●●●●

CREAMED TUNA

Makes 1 serving.

3 oz. canned or cooked tuna
1 1/2 c. frozen cauliflower, cooked and drained
1/3 c. instant nonfat dry milk
onion flakes
salt and pepper to taste

Cook together in a nonstick pan.

One serving counts as:	Fruit	Milk ●	Bread
Freedom to Choose Calories:	Vegetable ●●●	Fat	Protein ●●●

TUNA STUFFED TOMATO

Makes 1 serving.

3 oz. canned or cooked tuna
1/2 c. cooked macaroni
1/2 c. diced celery
1 tsp. onion
2 tsp. diet mayonnaise
pimento for garnish
1 tomato

Combine first 5 ingredients. Stuff tomato with mixture and garnish with pimento.

One serving counts as:	Fruit	Milk	Bread ●
Freedom to Choose Calories:	Vegetable ●●	Fat ●	Protein ●●●

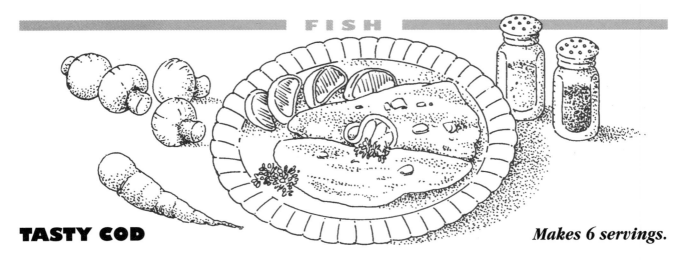

TASTY COD

Makes 6 servings.

1 1/2 lbs. frozen cod fillets
1/4 tsp. salt
1/4 tsp. pepper

Place frozen fish in a baking dish coated with nonstick cooking spray; lightly salt and pepper.

1 tsp. tarragon
1 Tbsp. lemon juice

Sprinkle with tarragon and lemon juice.

1 c. chopped mushrooms
1 1/2 c. thinly sliced carrots
1/2 c. celery
1 Tbsp. fresh chopped parsley
1 Tbsp. margarine

Add chopped vegetables and fresh parsley. Dot with margarine. Cover tightly. Bake at 350 degrees for 35-45 minutes.

One serving counts as:	Fruit	Milk	Bread
Freedom to Choose Calories:	Vegetable ●	Fat ◖	Protein ●●●

SALMON LOAF

Makes 4 servings.

12 oz. canned salmon, drained
4 slices bread, crumbed
1/2 c. evaporated skimmed milk OR 1/3 c. instant
    nonfat dry milk + 4 oz. water

In large bowl mix first 3 ingredients.

2 large eggs, beaten
2 Tbsp. minced onion
2 Tbsp. chopped parsley
1/4 tsp. salt
1/2 tsp. sage

Add remaining ingredients and blend. Pour mixture in loaf pan sprayed with nonstick cooking spray. Bake at 350 degrees for 35 minutes.

One serving counts as:	Fruit	Milk ◗	Bread ●
Freedom to Choose Calories:	Vegetable	Fat	Protein ●●●◖

FISH CHEESEBURGER

Makes 1 serving.

2 oz. cooked fish (tuna, etc.)
1 slice bread (not diet)
1/2 c. cooked asparagus, broccoli, etc.
1 oz. slice cheddar or American cheese

Mash well seasoned fish to a paste and spread on bread; cover with vegetable and top with cheese. Broil until cheese melts.

One serving counts as:	Fruit	Milk	Bread ●
Freedom to Choose Calories:	Vegetable ●	Fat	Protein ● ● ●

BAKED HADDOCK WITH MOUNTAIN YOGURT SAUCE

Makes 2 servings.

8 oz. fresh haddock (or other firm-fleshed white fish)
1/4 c. lemon juice

Preheat oven to 450 degrees (hot oven). Soak fish in lemon juice for 20 minutes; this will add flavor and promote whiteness.

1/2 tsp. salt, or to taste
1/8 tsp. pepper, or to taste

Pat dry with paper towel; season with salt and pepper.

Place on nonstick baking sheet. Cooking time should be determined by measuring the fish at the thickest part. Allow 10-12 minutes in the oven per inch of thickness. Do not overcook! Serve with sauce (below) on the side.

One serving counts as:	Fruit	Milk	Bread
Freedom to Choose Calories:	Vegetable	Fat	Protein ● ● ●

MOUNTAIN YOGURT SAUCE

Makes 2 servings.

1/2 c. plain lowfat yogurt
1 tsp. mayonnaise
1 tsp. lemon juice
3/4 tsp. curry (or to taste)
dash each of artificial sweetener, salt, pepper

Mix together and serve over fish (above).

One serving counts as:	Fruit	Milk ◖	Bread
Freedom to Choose Calories:	Vegetable	Fat ◖	Protein

ASPARAGUS TUNA BAKE

Makes 1 serving.

1 1/2 c. canned asparagus, cut
2 oz. canned or cooked tuna

Drain asparagus. Save 1/4 c. liquid and set aside. Place asparagus in bottom of 1 quart casserole. Add tuna.

1 oz. American cheese
1 slice bread (not diet)

Break up cheese and place evenly over tuna. Tear up bread and evenly place over cheese.

1/3 c. instant nonfat dry milk

Mix dry milk with reserved liquid and pour over bread.

Bake at 350 degrees until bread browns.

One serving counts as:	Fruit	Milk ●	Bread ●
Freedom to Choose Calories:	Vegetable ●●●	Fat	Protein ●●●

SALMON DELIGHT

Makes 1 serving.

3 oz. canned or cooked salmon
1/4 c. mushrooms
1/4 c. onion, diced
1/4 c. celery, diced
1 slice bread (not diet), broken into pieces
1/4 c. skim milk
salt and pepper to taste

Mix and cook all ingredients in a nonstick skillet sprayed with nonstick cooking spray over medium heat until celery is almost completely tender. Serve hot. Shape into patty on plate.

One serving counts as:	Fruit	Milk ◖	Bread ●
Freedom to Choose Calories:	Vegetable ●◖	Fat	Protein ●●●

GRILLED FLOUNDER FILLETS

Makes 4 servings.

1 lb. flounder fillets

2 medium limes
2 tsp. thyme
2 tsp. salt
1/2 tsp. pepper

Place flounder on sheet of aluminum foil.

Squeeze limes and pour juice over fish; sprinkle evenly with seasonings.

Grill on rack 5" from source of heat, 7 minutes on each side until fish flakes easily with fork.

One serving counts as:	Fruit	Milk	Bread
Freedom to Choose Calories:	Vegetable	Fat	Protein ●●●

HAWAIIAN BEACHCOMBER'S SALAD

Makes 2 servings.

6 oz. drained and flaked canned tuna
1/2 c. diced celery
2 Tbsp. pickle relish
1 small banana, sliced
1/2 c. pineapple tidbits and the juice that clings
1 Tbsp. & 1 tsp. diet mayonnaise
1/2 tsp. dry mustard
2 c. shredded lettuce

Combine all ingredients except lettuce; mix thoroughly and divide evenly into 2 large salad bowls holding shredded lettuce.

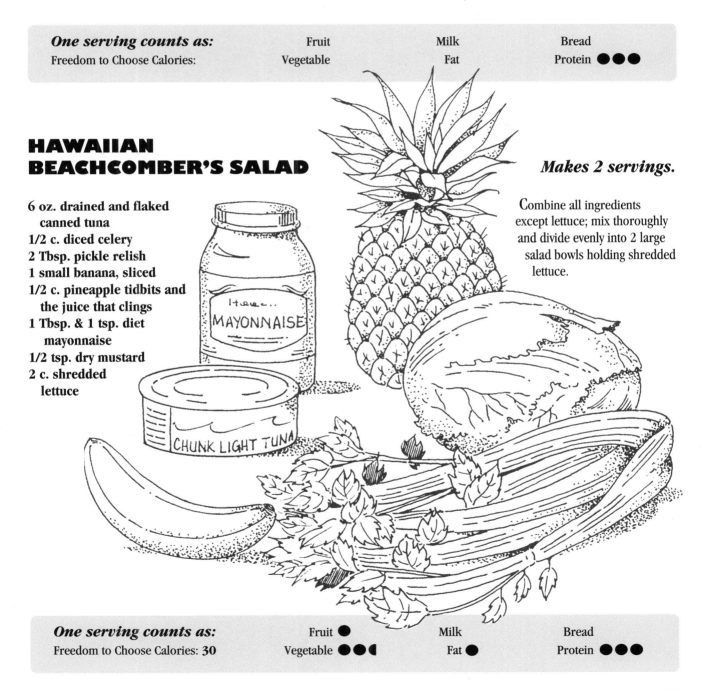

One serving counts as:	Fruit ●	Milk	Bread
Freedom to Choose Calories: 30	Vegetable ●●◗	Fat ●	Protein ●●●

FRUIT

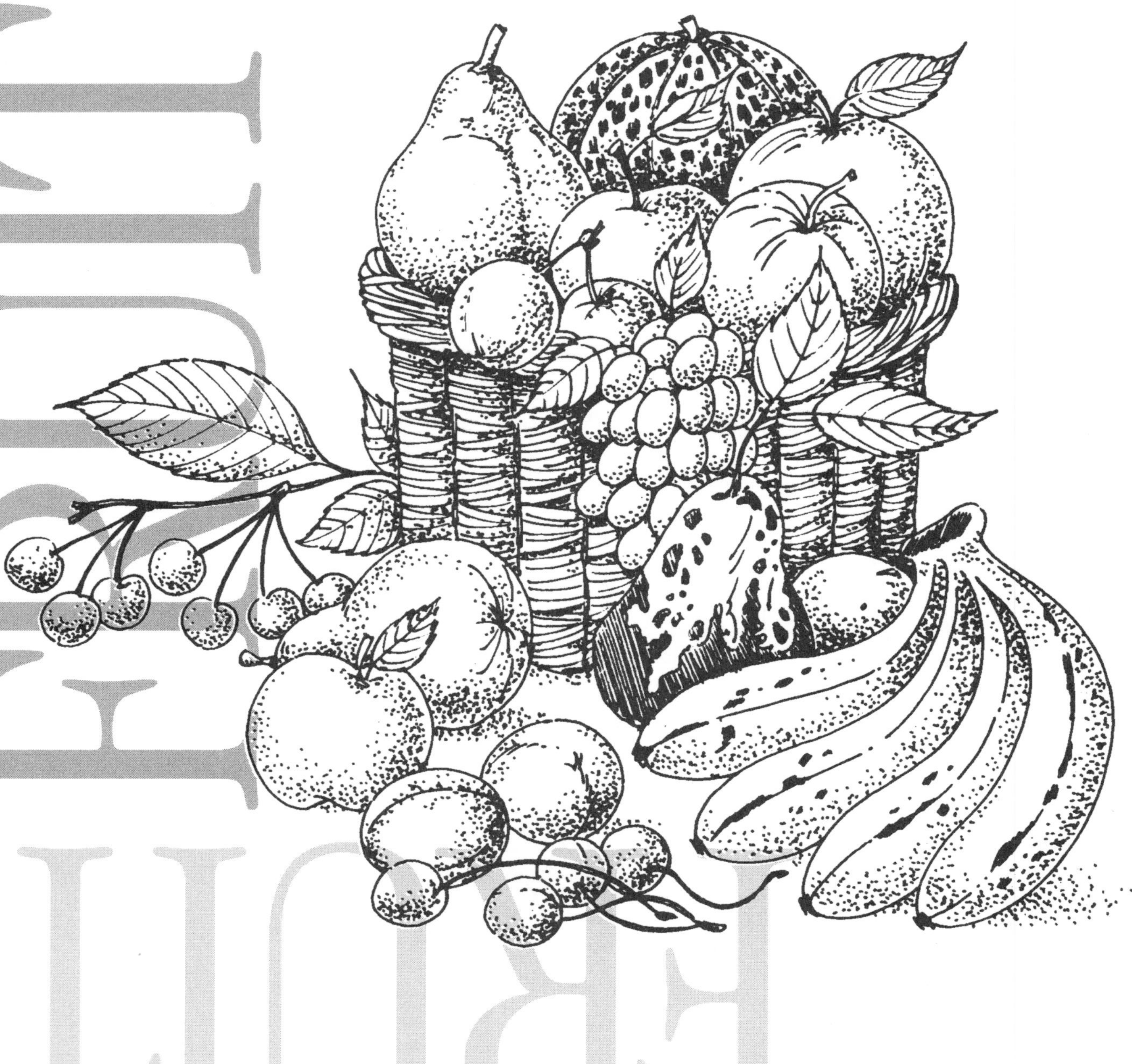

STRAWBERRY CHEESE BAVARIAN

Makes 2 servings.

1 1/3 c. cottage cheese

Make sour cream by pureeing cottage cheese in blender with just enough water (a Tbsp. or two) to start the blender.

1 envelope (1 Tbsp.) unflavored gelatin
1/4 c. cold water
3 pkts. Sweet N Low
1/4 tsp. salt

Sprinkle gelatin over 1/4 c. water in small saucepan to soften, then place over low heat, stirring constantly to dissolve gelatin. Remove from heat; stir in artificial sweetener and salt.

2 c. fresh or frozen strawberries
1/4 tsp. berry extract

Combine 1 c. of the berries and berry extract; mash lightly and add to gelatin mixture. Fold in the cottage cheese and pour into a wet 3-cup mold. Chill 2-3 hours or until firm. Unmold and garnish with reserved strawberries.

One serving counts as:	Fruit ●	Milk	Bread
Freedom to Choose Calories:	Vegetable	Fat	Protein ●●

APPLE PEANUT BUTTER DREAM

Makes 1 serving.

1/4 c. plain NONfat yogurt
1 Tbsp. peanut butter
1 Tbsp. raisins
1 small apple, diced
1 pkt. Equal
2 Tbsp. celery

Mix together and serve on lettuce leaves.

One serving counts as:	Fruit ●◖	Milk ◖	Bread
Freedom to Choose Calories:	Vegetable	Fat ●	Protein ●

MOLDED CRANBERRY WALDORF SALAD

Makes 4 servings.

2 c. low calorie cranberry juice

1 four-serving pkg. sugar-free strawberry gelatin
1/4 tsp. salt
2 small unpared apples, chopped
1/2 c. celery, chopped

Bring 1 c. cranberry juice to boil; stir into gelatin.

Add remaining juice and salt. Chill until partially set. Stir in apple and celery.

One serving counts as:	Fruit ●	Milk	Bread
Freedom to Choose Calories: 8	Vegetable ◗	Fat	Protein

CRANBERRY GELEE

Makes 4 servings.

1 envelope (1 Tbsp.) unflavored gelatin
1 1/4 c. water

2 c. raw cranberries
12 pkts. Equal (or to taste)

Soften gelatin in 1/4 c. of the water.

In saucepan, cook cranberries in remaining water until skins pop. Add gelatin, stirring to dissolve. Cool to lukewarm and add sweetener. Pour into mold. Chill until set.

One serving counts as:	Fruit ◖	Milk	Bread
Freedom to Choose Calories:	Vegetable	Fat	Protein

SWEET FRUIT 'N' NOODLE PUDDING

Makes 4 servings.

2 tsp. unsalted margarine, divided

Grease 1 qt. casserole with 1/2 tsp. margarine, set aside.

8 large prunes, pitted and diced
2 Tbsp. boiling water

In small bowl combine prunes and boiling water, set aside. Preheat oven to 400 degrees.

1 c. skim milk
2/3 c. cottage cheese
2 large eggs
3 pkts. Sweet N Low
1 tsp. vanilla extract
1/2 tsp. cinnamon

In blender container combine remaining 1 1/2 tsp. margarine with milk, cheese, eggs, artificial sweetener, vanilla, and cinnamon; process until smooth.

2 c. cooked noodles (medium width)

Pour into greased casserole; add noodles, prunes, and liquid that prunes were soaked in and stir until combined.

Bake until browned, 20-25 minutes. Remove from oven; let stand until set, about 10 minutes.

One serving counts as:	Fruit ●	Milk ◖	Bread ●
Freedom to Choose Calories:	Vegetable	Fat ◖	Protein ●

BAKED BANANA

Makes 1 serving.

1 small banana

Slice banana in half lengthwise. Place in individual baking dish.

2 Tbsp. fresh lemon juice
1 tsp. rum extract

Combine lemon juice and rum extract and pour over banana halves.

brown sugar substitute to equal 2 tsp. brown sugar
1 tsp. cinnamon
pinch each of ground cloves and nutmeg
1 tsp. diet margarine

Combine sugar substitute, cinnamon, cloves, and nutmeg. Sprinkle over banana surfaces. Bake at 350 degrees for 10 minutes. Melt margarine and drizzle over banana and place in oven for 30 seconds more.

One serving counts as:	Fruit ●	Milk	Bread
Freedom to Choose Calories:	Vegetable	Fat ◖	Protein

STRAWBERRY PUFF

Makes 1 serving.

1 large egg, separated
1 Tbsp. water
1 slice bread (not diet)

1/4 tsp. cream of tartar
2 pkts. Sweet N Low
1 c. fresh or frozen strawberries
1 tsp. cornstarch

Mix egg yolk with water. Dip bread into egg yolk mixture until completely absorbed. Place in a baking dish coated with nonstick cooking spray.

Beat egg white, cream of tartar, and 1 pkt. Sweet N Low until stiff. Spread over bread and bake at 350 degrees for 15 minutes. Cool.

Cook together strawberries, cornstarch, and 1 pkt. Sweet N Low until thickened. Cool and pour over bread.

One serving counts as:	Fruit ●	Milk	Bread ●
Freedom to Choose Calories: **10**	Vegetable	Fat	Protein ●

BLUEBERRY CRUMBLE

Makes 1 serving.

1/2 c. fresh or frozen blueberries
2 pkts. Sweet N Low
1 oz. grapenuts-like cereal
2 Tbsp. & 2 tsp. instant nonfat dry milk
dash nutmeg
1 Tbsp. diet margarine

Mix the blueberries with sweetener in a 10 oz. custard cup. Mix remaining ingredients until crumbly. Spoon over berries. Bake at 350 degrees for 20 minutes OR in microwave for 4 minutes.

One serving counts as:	Fruit ●	Milk ◖	Bread ●
Freedom to Choose Calories:	Vegetable	Fat ●◖	Protein

GRAPEFRUIT MERINGUE

Makes 1 serving.

1/2 medium grapefruit
1 large egg white
1/8 tsp. cream of tartar
dash salt
dash vanilla extract

Loosen pulp. Beat egg white with cream of tartar, salt, and vanilla until it stands in peaks. Sweeten with artificial sweetener if desired. Top grapefruit with egg white and place on foil pan. Bake at 350 degrees for 10-12 minutes.

One serving counts as:	Fruit ●	Milk	Bread
Freedom to Choose Calories: **17**	Vegetable	Fat	Protein

BANANA SPLIT PIE

Makes 4 servings.

8 graham cracker squares (2 1/2"), crushed
4 Tbsp. diet margarine
1 four-serving pkg. sugar-free vanilla pudding
1 small banana, sliced
1 c. crushed pineapple, drained
1 c. whipped topping

1st layer: Melt margarine in 8" pie plate. Add graham crackers and pat into bottom and sides of plate.
2nd layer: Pudding prepared with skim milk as directed on package.
3rd layer: Sliced banana.
4th layer: Drained crushed pineapple.
5th layer: Whipped topping.

Chill or can be frozen. Bananas will turn brown fast so eat soon after making.

One serving counts as:	Fruit ◗	Milk ●	Bread ●
Freedom to Choose Calories: **50**	Vegetable	Fat ● ◗	Protein

STRAWBERRY CHEESECAKE

Makes 1 serving.

1/4 c. cold water
1 envelope (1 Tbsp.) unflavored gelatin
1/4 c. hot water

Soften gelatin in cold water. Add hot water. Blend in blender to dissolve.

1/3 c. instant nonfat dry milk
2 pkts. Equal
1 tsp. vanilla extract
1/3 c. cottage cheese
1 c. fresh or frozen strawberries

Add dry milk, Equal, vanilla, cottage cheese, and strawberries. Blend together and refrigerate.

One serving counts as:	Fruit ●	Milk ●	Bread
Freedom to Choose Calories:	Vegetable	Fat	Protein ●

REFRIGERATOR APPLE BUTTER

Makes 4 servings.

2 tart small apples	Pare, core, and quarter apples.
2 c. water 3 pkts. Sweet N Low 1/4 tsp. cinnamon 1/8 tsp. allspice 1 1/2 tsp. unflavored gelatin 1/4 c. water	Combine in blender with water, sweetener, and spices. Blend until mixture is smooth. Cook over low heat until thickened, approximately 45 minutes. In blender container, sprinkle gelatin over 1/4 c. water. Transfer boiling apple mixture to blender; puree. Store in refrigerator, evenly divided into 4 small jars.

One serving counts as:	Fruit ◖	Milk	Bread
Freedom to Choose Calories:	Vegetable	Fat	Protein

TOFU SHAKE

Makes 2 servings.

6 oz. silken tofu 1 c. fresh or frozen strawberries 8 oz. diet red carbonated beverage	Blend together in blender.

One serving counts as:	Fruit ◖	Milk	Bread
Freedom to Choose Calories: **diet bev.**	Vegetable	Fat	Protein ●

FRUITED COTTAGE CHEESE MOLD

Makes 8 servings.

1 eight-serving pkg. sugar-free gelatin 1 c. boiling water	Dissolve gelatin in boiling water.
3/4 c. cold water 1 1/3 c. cottage cheese (pureed in blender) 2 c. sugar-free drained fruit	Add cold water. Chill until partially thickened. Fold in cottage cheese and fruit. Pour into 4-cup mold or 8 individual molds. Chill. Garnish with salad greens.

One serving counts as:	Fruit ◖	Milk	Bread
Freedom to Choose Calories: **8**	Vegetable	Fat	Protein ◖

APRICOT DREAMS

Makes 2 servings.

3 Tbsp. part-skim ricotta cheese
2 tsp. reduced calorie apricot spread (16 calories per 2 tsp.)

In small bowl combine cheese and apricot spread.

8 apricot halves

Arrange apricot halves cut side up on serving dish; using a spoon or pastry bag fitted with a star tip, top each apricot half with 1/8 of cheese mixture.

ground cinnamon (opt.)

Sprinkle with cinnamon. Cover loosely and refrigerate 30 minutes.

One serving counts as:	Fruit ●	Milk	Bread
Freedom to Choose Calories: 45	Vegetable	Fat	Protein

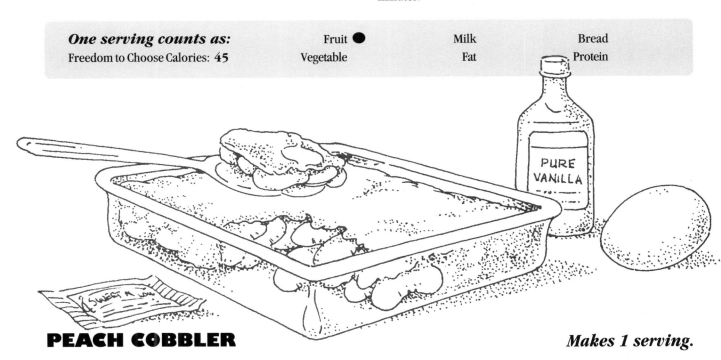

PEACH COBBLER

Makes 1 serving.

1 slice bread (not diet)

Break bread into small pieces and arrange in a 6" diameter baking dish.

1 medium peach, peeled and sliced
cinnamon

Arrange peach slices over bread and sprinkle with cinnamon.

1 c. skim milk, scalded
1 large egg
1/4 tsp. vanilla extract
4 pkts. Sweet N Low

Pour milk into blender; add egg, vanilla, and sweetener. Blend at high speed about 30 seconds.

Pour milk mixture over peach and bread, being careful not to overflow the dish. Lift a few pieces of the bread up to help form a top crust. Bake at 325 degrees for 25 minutes.

One serving counts as:	Fruit ●	Milk ●	Bread ●
Freedom to Choose Calories:	Vegetable	Fat	Protein ●

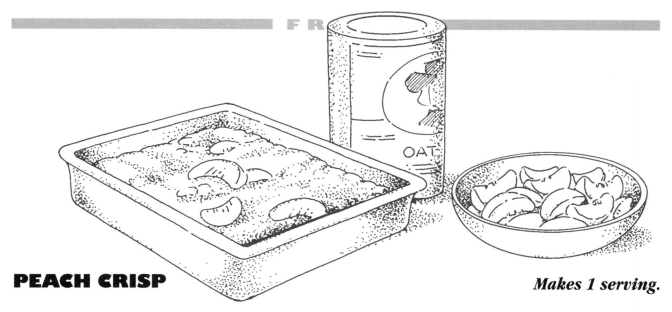

PEACH CRISP

Makes 1 serving.

1/2 c. sliced sugar-free peaches, any kind
1 pkt. Sweet N Low
1/2 tsp. melted margarine
1/8 tsp. cinnamon
dash salt

Place peaches, Sweet N Low, 1/2 tsp. margarine, cinnamon, and salt in a small baking dish that has been coated with nonstick cooking spray.

2 tsp. flour
1 tsp. margarine
1 oz. rolled oats

Combine remaining ingredients until crumbly. Sprinkle over peaches. Bake at 375 degrees for 10 minutes.

One serving counts as:	Fruit ●	Milk	Bread ●
Freedom to Choose Calories: **20**	Vegetable	Fat ●◖	Protein

APPLE RAISIN BROWN BETTY

Makes 4 servings.

4 small apples, pared, cored, and sliced

Layer apples in an 8" square nonstick baking pan.

1/2 c. water
1 Tbsp. cornstarch
1 tsp. cinnamon

Combine water, cornstarch, and cinnamon in a measuring cup. Stir to dissolve cornstarch; pour over apples.

2 slices raisin bread (not diet), crumbed
1 Tbsp. & 1 tsp. diet margarine

In a bowl combine bread crumbs and margarine. Mix until particles are the size of peas. Sprinkle over apples. Bake at 350 degrees for 40-45 minutes.

One serving counts as:	Fruit ●	Milk	Bread ◖
Freedom to Choose Calories: **8**	Vegetable	Fat ◖	Protein

BLUEBERRY FREEZE

Makes 1 serving.

1/2 c. frozen blueberries
1/2 c. skim milk
1 pkt. Equal

Combine all ingredients and stir until milk crystallizes.

One serving counts as:	Fruit ●	Milk ◖	Bread
Freedom to Choose Calories:	Vegetable	Fat	Protein

STRAWBERRY MOUSSE

Makes 4 servings.

1 four-serving pkg. sugar-free strawberry gelatin
3/4 c. boiling water

Mix gelatin and boiling water in blender at low speed until gelatin is dissolved, about 30 seconds.

1 c. ice cubes

Add ice; stir until partially melted.

1/2 c. thawed frozen whipped topping
1 c. sliced fresh or frozen strawberries

Add whipped topping and strawberries; blend well at highest speed, about 30 seconds. Pour into individual glasses. Chill 30 minutes. Garnish with strawberries.

One serving counts as:	Fruit ◀	Milk	Bread
Freedom to Choose Calories: **33**	Vegetable	Fat	Protein

BANANA SPLIT BREAKFAST

Makes 1 serving.

1 small banana, split in half lengthwise

Arrange banana in a banana split dish.

1/3 c. cottage cheese

Mound cottage cheese over banana halves.

2 tsp. reduced calorie strawberry jam (16 calories in 2 tsp.)

Melt strawberry jam briefly in microwave (5 seconds) and drizzle over top of cottage cheese.

1/2 tsp. sunflower seeds
lettuce as garnish (opt.)

Sprinkle sunflower seeds over all.

One serving counts as:	Fruit ●	Milk	Bread
Freedom to Choose Calories: **26**	Vegetable	Fat	Protein ●

UNBELIEVABLE LASAGNA

Makes 8 servings.

1 lb. ground turkey browned with 3/4 c. chopped onion and 1 garlic clove, minced; discard fat that cooks out of meat

Mix together: 4 c. tomato sauce
1/8 tsp. crushed red pepper
1/4 tsp. chili powder
2 tsp. dried parsley leaves
1 tsp. oregano
1 tsp. basil leaves
1/4 tsp. paprika

Mix together: 8 oz. shredded mozzarella cheese
1 1/3 c. cottage cheese
1/2 c. grated parmesan cheese

8 oz. lasagna noodles, UNCOOKED

In 13 x 9 x 2" baking dish, spread about 1 cup sauce mixture.

Arrange a layer of 3 uncooked lasagna strips; top with some sauce mixture, cheese mixture, and ground turkey mixture.

Repeat twice, ending with cheese mixture and making sure all lasagna pieces are covered with sauce by gently pressing into sauce.

Bake at 350 degrees for 45 -55 minutes. For moister lasagna, add a small amount of water to sauce.

One serving counts as:	Fruit	Milk	Bread ●
Freedom to Choose Calories: **55**	Vegetable ◖	Fat	Protein ●●●

FOWL CHEESE

Makes 2 servings.

2   4 oz. skinned and boned chicken breasts

2 oz. mozzarella cheese
1/4 tsp. pepper
1/4 tsp. salt

1 slice white or wheat bread (not diet), toasted and crumbed

Preheat oven to 350 degrees. Put chicken between pieces of waxed paper and pound with iron skillet or rolling pin to flatten.

Salt and pepper and put 1 ounce of cheese on each portion. Roll chicken and secure with string or toothpicks.

Wet outside with water, roll in bread crumbs. Pour extra crumbs over top. Place on flat pan. Bake for 45 minutes.

One serving counts as:	Fruit	Milk	Bread ◖
Freedom to Choose Calories:	Vegetable	Fat	Protein ●●●●

PEPPER MATES

Makes 2 servings.

2 large green peppers

Slice off tops of green peppers and remove seeds. Parboil peppers in boiling salted water 5 minutes; drain. Set aside.

1/2 lb. turkey breakfast sausage
1/2 c. onion, chopped

Brown sausage and onion; cook until tender. Pour off drippings.

1 c. chopped tomatoes
1 c. cooked rice
2 tsp. Worcestershire sauce
salt, pepper, and parsley

Add tomatoes, rice, and Worcestershire sauce; season to taste with salt and pepper. Simmer 5 minutes.

1 oz. shredded sharp cheddar cheese

Stuff peppers with mixture and place in 1 qt. casserole dish. Pack any extra stuffing around peppers. Bake at 350 degrees for 30 minutes. Top with cheese. Garnish with parsley.

One serving counts as:	Fruit	Milk	Bread ●
Freedom to Choose Calories:	Vegetable ●●●◑	Fat	Protein ●●●◑

CABBAGE MEAL IN ONE

Makes 4 servings.

1 small head of cabbage, coarsely chopped

Place cabbage in casserole dish sprayed with nonstick cooking spray.

1 lb. ground turkey, browned and drained
1 c. hot water
1 c. chopped onion
1/2 c. raw rice
1 tsp. salt
1/2 tsp. oregano
2 cups canned tomatoes

Mix other ingredients and add to cabbage. Cover and bake at 350 degrees for 1 1/2 hours.

One serving counts as:	Fruit	Milk	Bread ◑
Freedom to Choose Calories:	Vegetable ●●●	Fat	Protein ●●●

PIZZA CASSEROLE

Makes 4 servings.

1 lb. turkey breakfast sausage
1/2 c. mushrooms, sliced
1/2 c. onion, diced
1/2 c. green peppers, diced

1 c. tomato juice
1/4 tsp. basil
1/2 tsp. oregano

8 slices Weight Watcher's mozzarella cheese

Brown meat with onion, mushrooms, and green peppers; drain.

Stir in tomato juice, basil, and oregano. Put 1/2 mixture in 1 1/2 quart casserole dish sprayed with nonstick cooking spray.

Cover with 4 slices cheese; add remaining mixture and cover with remaining cheese. Bake at 350 degrees for 30-40 minutes.

One serving counts as:	Fruit	Milk	Bread
Freedom to Choose Calories:	Vegetable ●◖	Fat	Protein ●●●●

REALLY GOOD GOULASH

Makes 2 servings.

6 oz. cooked ground turkey, crumbled
brown sugar substitute to equal 1 1/2 Tbsp. brown
    sugar
1 Tbsp. onion flakes
salt and pepper
1 c. green beans
1 c. cooked macaroni
1/2 c. tomato juice
1 Tbsp. vinegar
1 1/2 tsp. Worcestershire sauce
1/2 tsp. prepared mustard

Mix together and bake at 350 degrees for 30 minutes or in microwave until hot.

One serving counts as:	Fruit	Milk	Bread ●
Freedom to Choose Calories:	Vegetable ●●	Fat	Protein ●●●

CHILI BEEF DINNER

Makes 4 servings.

1 lb. ground beef or turkey, browned and drained
1/2 c. chopped onion
1 medium clove garlic, crushed
1 tsp. salt

1 Tbsp. chili powder
1   16 oz. can tomatoes, cut up
1   6 oz. can tomato paste
2 c. water

1 c. elbow macaroni, uncooked

In large skillet combine ground meat, onion, garlic, and salt.

Add chili powder, tomatoes, tomato paste, and water. Bring to boil.

Gradually stir in macaroni so mixture continues to boil. Cover and simmer 15 minutes, stirring occasionally. Remove cover and simmer 10 minutes or until sauce is thickened and macaroni is tender.

One serving counts as:
Freedom to Choose Calories:

Fruit
Vegetable ●◖

Milk
Fat

Bread ●
Protein ●●●

CHICKEN CHOW MEIN

Makes 2 servings.

2 c. celery, chopped fine
2 Tbsp. dry onion
1 c. water
Stir fry until water is gone.

Add:
1 chicken bouillon cube
2 c. bean sprouts, drained
1/2 c. mushrooms
2 Tbsp. soy sauce
6 oz. cooked chicken, diced
1 c. water

Heat gently. Serve with English mustard (this is HOT): mix dry mustard with water to form paste, let stand 10 minutes.

One serving counts as:
Freedom to Choose Calories: 5

Fruit
Vegetable ●●●●◖

Milk
Fat

Bread
Protein ●●●

STIR FRY CHICKEN AND VEGETABLES

Makes 4 servings.

1 lb. skinned and boned chicken thighs

Cut chicken into bite-size pieces.

1 Tbsp. & 1 tsp. cooking oil
1 garlic clove, minced

In large frying pan, place oil and heat to medium high temperature. Add chicken, garlic, and stir fry about 3 minutes or until chicken loses its pink color.

1 1/2 c. broccoli, chopped
1 1/2 c. carrots, thinly sliced
1 1/2 c. celery, diagonally sliced
1/2 c. onion, chopped

Add carrots; then broccoli, celery, and onion; continue cooking about 5 minutes, stirring constantly through entire process.

1/4 tsp. pepper
1 Tbsp. soy sauce
1/4 c. chicken broth
1   16 oz. can bean sprouts, drained
1 c. sliced mushrooms
2 c. cooked rice

Sprinkle with pepper and soy sauce. Pour chicken broth over contents in frying pan. When liquid begins to boil, add bean sprouts and mushrooms.

Heat about 2 minutes more. Vegetables should remain crisp; do not overcook. Serve over rice.

One serving counts as:	Fruit	Milk	Bread ●
Freedom to Choose Calories:	Vegetable ●●●●	Fat ●	Protein ●●●

SECOND TIME TURKEY

Makes 2 servings.

4 oz. cooked turkey
2 tsp. dried onion flakes
1 pkt. chicken broth & seasoning mix
2 c. boiling water
1/2 c. green peas
1/2 c. cabbage
1/2 c. sliced carrots
3 oz. diced potatoes
salt and pepper to taste

Mix together and simmer until vegetables are tender.

One serving counts as:	Fruit	Milk	Bread ●
Freedom to Choose Calories: **5**	Vegetable ●	Fat	Protein ●●

MEATBALLS

Makes 4 servings.

1 lb. ground turkey
2 slices bread (not diet), crumbed
4 tsp. dehydrated chopped onion
3 Tbsp. plain, NONfat yogurt
1/4 tsp. basil
1 pkt. beef broth & seasoning mix
1 large egg, beaten
salt and pepper to taste
1/2 tsp. oregano
1/2 tsp. sage
1 tsp. soy sauce

Combine all ingredients and shape into small meatballs. Brown in 1 tablespoon hot oil. Remove to plate.

Sauce: In skillet, combine:
2 pkts. beef broth & seasoning mix
1 c. boiling water
1 tsp. soy sauce
1/4 tsp. basil
5 Tbsp. plain, NONfat yogurt

Bring to boil. Reduce heat and mix together 3 Tbsp. water and 1 Tbsp. cornstarch. Add meatballs. Cook on low heat 10-20 minutes. Add yogurt and stir just until heated through but do not boil.

One serving counts as:	Fruit	Milk ◗	Bread ●
Freedom to Choose Calories: **15**	Vegetable	Fat ◖	Protein ●●●◗

SLOPPY JOES

Makes 4 servings.

1 lb. ground turkey

1 pkg. SLOPPY JOE SEASONING (see below)
1/2 c. water
1 (8 oz.) can tomato sauce
4 hamburger buns, toasted

Seasoning Mix:
1 Tbsp. instant minced onion
1 tsp. green pepper flakes
1 tsp. salt
1 tsp. cornstarch
1/2 tsp. instant minced garlic
1/4 tsp. dry mustard
1/4 tsp. celery seed
1/4 tsp. chili powder

Brown turkey in medium skillet. Drain to remove fat.

Add SLOPPY JOE SEASONING MIX, water, and tomato sauce. Bring to a boil. Reduce heat and simmer 10 minutes, stirring occasionally. Serve over toasted buns.

Combine all ingredients. Spoon onto 6" square of aluminum foil and fold to make air-tight. Label. Store in cool, dry place. Use within 6 months. Makes 1 pkg. (3 Tbsp.).

One serving counts as:	Fruit	Milk	Bread ●●
Freedom to Choose Calories: 3	Vegetable ◖	Fat	Protein ●●●

TACOS

Makes 8 servings.

1 lb. ground turkey

1/2 c. water
1 pkg. TACO SEASONING MIX (see below)
8   6" corn or flour tortillas

Seasoning Mix:
1 tsp. instant minced onion
1 tsp. salt
1 tsp. chili powder
1/2 tsp. cornstarch
1/2 tsp. crushed dry red pepper
1/2 tsp. instant minced garlic
1/4 tsp. dried oregano
1/2 tsp. ground cumin

Brown turkey in medium skillet. Drain to remove fat.

Add water and TACO SEASONING MIX. Reduce heat and simmer 10 minutes, stirring occasionally.

Combine all ingredients in a small bowl until evenly distributed. Spoon mixture onto a 6" square of aluminum foil and fold to make air-tight. Label. Store in a cool, dry place. Use within 6 months. Makes 1 pkg. (about 2 Tbsp.).

One serving counts as:	Fruit	Milk	Bread ●
Freedom to Choose Calories:	Vegetable	Fat	Protein ●◖

FRUIT ICE CREAM

Makes 1 serving.

3/4 c. buttermilk
1/4 c. crushed pineapple
artificial sweetener (Equal) to taste
small amount of vanilla, coconut, or other
    flavoring

Mix well and freeze until slushy. It tastes like ice cream.

One serving counts as:	Fruit ◖	Milk ●	Bread
Freedom to Choose Calories:	Vegetable	Fat	Protein

MILK FROTH

Makes 1 serving.

1 c. cold dietetic carbonated beverage (raspberry,
    orange, black cherry, cherry-cola, etc.)
1/2 c. cold skim milk

Combine in blender; process at high speed for 3 minutes.
Pour into tall glass over ice and serve immediately.

One serving counts as:	Fruit	Milk ◖	Bread
Freedom to Choose Calories: **diet bev.**	Vegetable	Fat	Protein

STRAWBERRY ICE CREAM

Makes 1 serving.

3/4 c. skim milk
1 c. frozen strawberries
1 tsp. vanilla extract
2 or 3 pkts. Equal

Blend in blender until texture of ice cream and serve.

One serving counts as:	Fruit ●	Milk ◕	Bread
Freedom to Choose Calories:	Vegetable	Fat	Protein

PEACH NECTAR

Makes 1 serving.

1 medium peach
1/2 c. evaporated skimmed milk
2 Tbsp. club soda

Mix ingredients in blender until everything is smooth; use immediately.

One serving counts as:	Fruit ●	Milk ●	Bread
Freedom to Choose Calories:	Vegetable	Fat	Protein

LEMON ICE CREAM

Makes 8 servings.

2 tsp. unflavored gelatin
1/2 c. evaporated skimmed milk

Sprinkle gelatin over 1/2 c. milk in small saucepan. Let soften 5 minutes. Heat, stirring constantly until gelatin dissolves, about 3 minutes. Remove from heat. Cool.

12 pkts. Equal
1 pkt. low calorie whipped topping mix (D-Zerta)
1/3 c. cold lemon juice
3 Tbsp. cold evaporated skimmed milk

Add Equal. Prepare whipped topping according to package directions, substituting lemon juice and 3 Tbsp. milk for water. Whip 10 minutes or until thick and fluffy.

2 large egg whites

Whip egg whites until soft peaks form. Combine whipped topping and gelatin mixtures; fold in egg whites. Freeze 3 to 4 hours until firm. Scoop into dessert dishes. Best when used within 3 days.

One serving counts as:	Fruit	Milk	Bread
Freedom to Choose Calories: 64	Vegetable	Fat	Protein

PINA COLADA

Makes 1 serving.

1/3 c. instant nonfat dry milk
1/2 c. water
1 pkt. Equal
1/4 c. pineapple (canned in its own juice)
1/4 tsp. or more coconut extract
1/4 tsp. rum flavoring

Put ingredients in blender and mix for about 30 seconds. Serve over ice cubes.

One serving counts as:	Fruit ◗	Milk ●	Bread
Freedom to Choose Calories:	Vegetable	Fat	Protein

MILK SHERBET

Makes 2 servings.

1/3 c. instant nonfat dry milk OR 1/2 c. evaporated skimmed milk
12 fluid ounces dietetic carbonated beverage (any flavor)

Combine milk and carbonated beverage in bowl. Mix thoroughly. Pour into a shallow pan and freeze to a mush, 40-60 minutes. Serve at once, or transfer to bowl and beat rapidly until smooth and creamy. Return to pan; freeze. Defrost in refrigerator 15-30 minutes before serving, so sherbet can be spooned out.

One serving counts as:	Fruit	Milk ◖	Bread
Freedom to Choose Calories: **diet bev.**	Vegetable	Fat	Protein

BUTTERY MILK

Makes 1 cup.

1 c. lukewarm skim milk
1 Tbsp. lemon juice
dash of imitation butter flavoring
salt

Combine ingredients; let stand 5 minutes, then beat with rotary beater. May be used in recipes as substitute for commercial buttermilk, but count it as regular skim milk.

One cup counts as:	Fruit	Milk ●	Bread
Freedom to Choose Calories:	Vegetable	Fat	Protein

EGGLESS NOG

Makes 1 serving.

1/3 c. water
1/3 c. instant nonfat dry milk
1/4 tsp. rum extract
1/4 tsp. vanilla extract
dash nutmeg
4 ice cubes, crushed
1 pkt. Equal

Place all ingredients in blender and blend at low speed. Serve immediately.

One serving counts as:	Fruit	Milk ●	Bread
Freedom to Choose Calories:	Vegetable	Fat	Protein

STRAWBERRY YOGURT FROST

Makes 1 serving.

1 c. frozen strawberries
1 c. plain, NONfat yogurt
1 tsp. vanilla extract
3 pkts. Equal

Combine all ingredients in blender container. Blend well until thick.

One serving counts as:	Fruit ●	Milk ●	Bread
Freedom to Choose Calories:	Vegetable	Fat	Protein

FROZEN FUDGE BARS

Makes 1 serving.

1 oz. oatmeal, dry
1 Tbsp. peanut butter
1 pkt. sugar-free chocolate shake mix
1 Tbsp. raisins
1 tsp. honey
3 Tbsp. water

Mix all ingredients together. Drop by teaspoonful or shape into patties and freeze.

One serving counts as:	Fruit ◖	Milk ●	Bread ●
Freedom to Choose Calories: 20	Vegetable	Fat ●	Protein ●

"ICE CREAM SANDWICH"

Makes 1 serving.

2 2 1/2" square graham crackers
1/2 c. frozen dietetic dessert

Place frozen dietetic dessert between graham crackers. Wrap in plastic wrap and freeze.

One serving counts as:	Fruit	Milk	Bread ●
Freedom to Choose Calories: **frozen dessert**	Vegetable	Fat	Protein

YOGURT WHIP

Makes 4 servings.

1 four-serving pkg. sugar-free cherry gelatin
1/4 tsp. nutmeg
1 c. plain, NONfat yogurt

Add 1 c. boiling water to gelatin and nutmeg; stir to dissolve.

Add 1 c. cold water. Chill until slightly thickened.

Add yogurt and beat with rotary beater until light and fluffy (mixture may be thin). Chill in individual serving dishes until set.

One serving counts as:	Fruit	Milk ◗	Bread
Freedom to Choose Calories: **8**	Vegetable	Fat	Protein

CHOCOLATE PEANUT BUTTER SLURPIE

Makes 1 serving.

1/2 c. ice water
1 pkt. sugar-free chocolate shake mix
1 1/2 tsp. peanut butter
3 large ice cubes

Pour water into blender; add shake mix and peanut butter. Cover; process at low speed, adding ice cubes one at a time. Process at highest speed 60 seconds or until thickened and ice cubes are completely processed.

One serving counts as:	Fruit	Milk ●	Bread
Freedom to Choose Calories:	Vegetable	Fat ◖	Protein ◖

FUDGESICLE

Makes 4 servings.

2 pkts. sugar-free chocolate shake mix
1 c. cold water

Combine in blender 30 seconds. Pour into 4 small paper cups. Freeze for 40 minutes. Stir and add sticks; freeze until firm.

One serving counts as:	Fruit	Milk ◖	Bread
Freedom to Choose Calories:	Vegetable	Fat	Protein

VANILLA SHAKE

Makes 1 serving.

1/2 c. skim milk
3 pkts. Equal
3 ice cubes
1 tsp. vanilla extract

Combine all ingredients in blender. Blend at high speed until smooth. Serve immediately.

One serving counts as:	Fruit	Milk ◖	Bread
Freedom to Choose Calories:	Vegetable	Fat	Protein

HAPPY PINEAPPLE SHAKE

Makes 1 serving.

1/3 c. instant nonfat dry milk
1/2 c. pineapple (packed in its own juice)
1 tsp. pineapple extract
8 oz. diet cream soda
3-4 ice cubes

Combine all ingredients in blender. Blend for 60 seconds or until ice is crushed.

One serving counts as:	Fruit ●	Milk ●	Bread
Freedom to Choose Calories: **diet soda**	Vegetable	Fat	Protein

CHOCOLATE CREAM SODA

Makes 1 serving.

1/2 c. skim milk
1 pkt. sugar-free chocolate shake mix
3 large ice cubes
1/4 c. club soda

Pour milk into blender; add shake mix. Cover; process at low speed, adding ice cubes one at a time. Process at highest speed 60 seconds or until thickened and ice cubes are completely processed. Pour into a tall glass. Add club soda; gently stir.

One serving counts as:	Fruit	Milk ●◖	Bread
Freedom to Choose Calories:	Vegetable	Fat	Protein

RICE LIKE PUDDING

Makes 2 servings.

1/4 c. cold water
1 envelope (1 Tbsp.) unflavored gelatin
1/4 c. boiling water

Pour cold water in blender. Sprinkle in gelatin. Add boiling water; blend.

1/2 tsp. vanilla extract
2/3 c. instant nonfat dry milk
2 pkts. Equal

Add remaining ingredients, except apple and ice. Blend until smooth.

3 ice cubes

Add ice and continue blending until smooth.

1 small apple, grated

Fold in apple.

One serving counts as:	Fruit ◗	Milk ●	Bread
Freedom to Choose Calories:	Vegetable	Fat	Protein

MILKY FUDGE BARS

Makes 4 servings.

1 1/3 c. instant nonfat dry milk
1 Tbsp. & 1 tsp. cocoa

In a small bowl combine milk and cocoa and set aside.

1/3 c. water
1 pkt. Equal
1 tsp. chocolate extract
1/2 tsp. lemon extract
1/2 tsp. vanilla extract
1/2 tsp. imitation butter flavor extract

Prepare syrup with remaining ingredients and mix well. Stir into milk mixture until blended. Let stand 5 minutes. Divide into 4 servings on foil coated with nonstick cooking spray. Freeze 1 hour.

One serving counts as:	Fruit	Milk ●	Bread
Freedom to Choose Calories: 5	Vegetable	Fat	Protein

LEGAL FUDGE

Makes 1 serving.

1/3 c. instant nonfat dry milk
2 tsp. cocoa
1-2 pkts. Equal
1/4 tsp. vanilla extract
enough water to make fudge consistency

Mix together and form into balls. Chill for 10 minutes.

One serving counts as:	Fruit	Milk ●	Bread
Freedom to Choose Calories: **10**	Vegetable	Fat	Protein

ORANGE MILK FREEZE

Makes 1 serving.

1/3 c. instant nonfat dry milk
1/2 c. ice cold orange juice
2 pkts. Equal
1/2 tsp. vanilla extract

Combine all ingredients. Beat at high speed with electric mixer until mixture stands in peaks. Spoon into pint container. Freeze until firm.

One serving counts as:	Fruit ●	Milk ●	Bread
Freedom to Choose Calories:	Vegetable	Fat	Protein

WEIGH TO WIN SNICKER BARS

Makes 1 serving.

1 small banana, mashed
1 Tbsp. peanut butter
1 pkt. sugar-free chocolate shake mix
1 oz. grapenuts-like cereal

Mix ingredients in order given. Spray two paper muffin cups with nonstick cooking spray and divide mixture evenly (or wrap mixture in plastic wrap). Freeze. Enjoy these treats while frozen!

One serving counts as:	Fruit ●	Milk ●	Bread ●
Freedom to Choose Calories:	Vegetable	Fat ●	Protein ●

COCONUT MACAROON COOKIES

Makes 4 servings.

1 1/3 c. instant nonfat dry milk
2 small apples, peeled, cored, and grated (about 3/4 cup)
brown sugar substitute to equal 6 Tbsp. brown sugar
1/2 tsp. cinnamon
1/2 tsp. coconut extract

Combine all ingredients in mixing bowl; mix thoroughly. Drop by teaspoonful onto nonstick cookie sheet. Makes about 24 cookies. Bake at 350 degrees for 18 minutes. Store in a tightly covered container.

One serving counts as:	Fruit ◖	Milk ●	Bread
Freedom to Choose Calories:	Vegetable	Fat	Protein

SUNSHINE ORANGE CAKE

Makes 6 servings.

6 slices white bread (not diet)

Heat oven to 350 degrees. In blender, make bread into crumbs.

6 oz. concentrated orange juice, undiluted
6 large eggs
2 tsp. baking soda

Add orange juice, eggs, and soda, blending slowly at first. Batter will foam up but go down as beating continues. Gradually increase speed.

1/4 tsp. salt
1 tsp. orange extract
8 pkts. Sweet N Low
2 c. instant nonfat dry milk

Add remaining ingredients in order given. Blend about 3 minutes or until smooth. Pour into bundt pan coated with nonstick cooking spray. Bake 37-40 minutes or until golden brown.

One serving counts as:	Fruit ●	Milk ●	Bread ●
Freedom to Choose Calories:	Vegetable	Fat	Protein ●

VEGETABLES

VEGETABLES

VEGETABLES

LAYER SALAD

Makes 2 servings.

3 c. cut up lettuce
1/2 c. diced onion
4 oz. Canadian bacon, broiled and diced
1 oz. cheddar cheese, shredded

Layer first four ingredients in order given.

1/4 c. plain, lowfat yogurt
4 tsp. diet mayonnaise
1 pkt. Equal

Mix together yogurt, mayonnaise, and Equal. Spread evenly over top of salad. Cover and refrigerate overnight. Mix just before serving.

One serving counts as:	Fruit	Milk ◖	Bread
Freedom to Choose Calories:	Vegetable ●●●◖	Fat ●	Protein ●●

CARROT AND PINEAPPLE MOLD

Makes 1 serving.

1 envelope (1 Tbsp.) unflavored gelatin
1/4 c. water
1/4 c. hot water

Soften gelatin in water; stir in hot water to dissolve gelatin.

1/2 c. crushed pineapple canned in its own juice (not drained)
1/2 c. grated carrots
2 tsp. lemon juice
1/2 tsp. salt

Add rest of ingredients and pour into small wet mold.

Refrigerate until set. To unmold, dip outside of mold in very warm water almost to the top, run a knife around the inside, place serving plate upside down on top of mold, and invert.

One serving counts as:	Fruit ●	Milk	Bread
Freedom to Choose Calories:	Vegetable ●	Fat	Protein

WHIPPED CAULIFLOWER

Makes 1 serving.

1/2 c. cauliflower, cooked in chicken bouillon
1 tsp. margarine
salt and white pepper to taste
nutmeg (opt.)

Combine all ingredients and mix with fork or hand mixer.

One serving counts as:	Fruit		Milk		Bread	
Freedom to Choose Calories:	Vegetable ●		Fat ●		Protein	

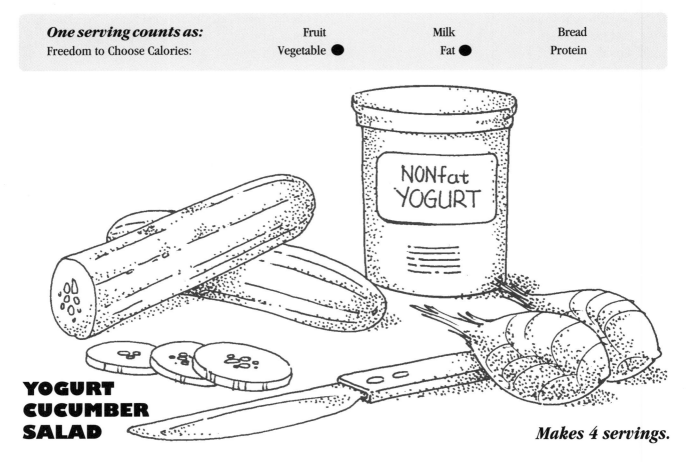

YOGURT CUCUMBER SALAD

Makes 4 servings.

1 1/2 c. thinly sliced cucumber
1/2 c. thinly sliced red onion
1/2 c. plain, NONfat yogurt
4 pkts. Equal
1/2 tsp. salt
1/8 tsp. pepper

Combine cucumber and onion slices in a bowl.

Combine remaining ingredients and pour over slices.

Toss. Serve immediately.

One serving counts as:	Fruit		Milk		Bread	
Freedom to Choose Calories: 13	Vegetable ●		Fat		Protein	

CHEESE AND POTATO RAGOUT

Makes 1 serving.

3 oz. potato, boiled and diced
1/2 c. mushrooms
salt and pepper
1/2 c. skim milk
2 oz. hard cheese
1 c. broccoli, cooked
paprika on top

Combine ingredients and bake at 350 degrees until bubbly.

One serving counts as:	Fruit	Milk ◖	Bread ●
Freedom to Choose Calories:	Vegetable ●●●	Fat	Protein ●●

CREAMY CARROT SOUP

Makes 4 servings.

1 c. chicken broth
1 Tbsp. snipped chives
1/2 tsp. celery salt
4 c. sliced carrots

Combine broth, chives, and celery salt in a saucepan. Bring to a boil; add carrots; simmer 10 minutes or until carrots are just tender. Transfer to blender; run at medium speed 60 seconds or until mixture is smooth. Return to saucepan.

1 c. evaporated skimmed milk
1 tsp. butter flavoring
1/2 pkt. Sweet N Low

Add milk, butter flavoring, and Sweet N Low. Cook over low heat, stirring occasionally for 5 minutes or until heated through.

One serving counts as:	Fruit	Milk ◖	Bread
Freedom to Choose Calories: **10**	Vegetable ●●	Fat	Protein

TOMATO SOUP

Makes 1 serving.

1 c. tomato juice
dash garlic powder
dash minced parsley

Combine all ingredients in saucepan. Bring to a boil and serve hot in a colorful mug.

One serving counts as:	Fruit	Milk	Bread
Freedom to Choose Calories:	Vegetable ●●	Fat	Protein

STIR FRY VEGETABLES

Makes 4 servings.

1 Tbsp. & 1 tsp. vegetable oil
2 c. shredded cabbage
1 c. shredded carrots
1/2 c. chopped fresh mushrooms
1/2 c. chopped onion
ginger to taste

Heat oil in a skillet. Add vegetables. Stir about 5 minutes using medium high heat or until tender crisp.

soy sauce

Sprinkle on some soy sauce and serve hot.

One serving counts as:	Fruit		Milk		Bread	
Freedom to Choose Calories:	Vegetable ●●		Fat ●		Protein	

SUMMER SLAW

Makes 12 servings.

6 c. thinly sliced cabbage
1/2 c. green pepper
1/4 c. vinegar
2 Tbsp. oil
1 Tbsp. sugar
salt and pepper to taste
Mrs. Dash to taste
1 radish to garnish

Toss all ingredients except radish and let stand at room temperature 1 hour. Do not refrigerate.

Note: *Refrigerate any leftovers.*

One serving counts as:	Fruit		Milk		Bread	
Freedom to Choose Calories: 5	Vegetable ●		Fat ◖		Protein	

GREEN BEAN CASSEROLE

Makes 1 serving.

1/2 c. onion, sliced
3/4 c. frozen French style green beans, cooked and drained

Brown onions in a hot nonstick skillet. Layer small casserole with onions and beans.

1/4 c. evaporated skimmed milk
1/4 c. canned mushrooms, drained
1 pkt. instant chicken broth & seasoning mix
garlic to taste

Combine remaining ingredients in a blender until smooth. Pour mixture over beans and onions and bake at 350 degrees for 20 minutes or until thoroughly heated.

One serving counts as:	Fruit		Milk ◖		Bread	
Freedom to Choose Calories: 10	Vegetable ●●●		Fat		Protein	

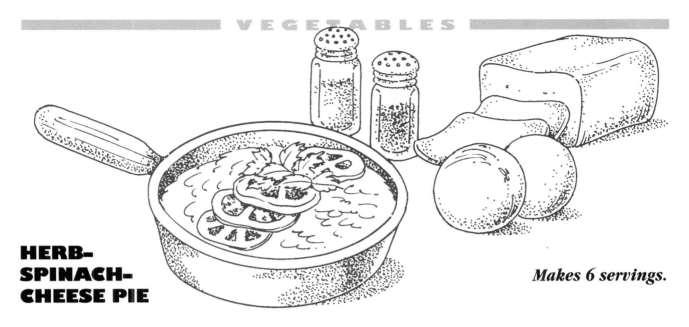

HERB-SPINACH-CHEESE PIE

Makes 6 servings.

1   9" pie shell, baked and cooled (recipe below)
3 large eggs
1 1/2 c. skim milk
1/2 tsp. Italian seasoning
1/4 tsp. salt
1/8 tsp. pepper

2 c. frozen chopped spinach, thawed and excess liquid
    squeezed out
1/2 c. chopped onion
6 oz. mozzarella cheese, shredded
1 c. sliced tomato

Combine eggs, milk, Italian seasoning, salt, and pepper.

Add spinach, onion, and 3/4 c. of cheese. Pour into pie shell. Top with tomato slices and remaining cheese.

Bake at 350 degrees for 50 minutes or until knife inserted near center comes out clean. Let stand for 10 minutes.

One serving counts as:	Fruit	Milk ◖	Bread ◖
Freedom to Choose Calories:	Vegetable ●	Fat	Protein ●◖

9" PIE CRUST

Makes 6 servings.

3 slices bread (not diet), toasted and made into
    crumbs
1/4 c. water
1/2 tsp. vanilla extract
2 pkts. Sweet N Low

Place bread crumbs into mixing bowl. Add water, vanilla, and sweetener. Mix to smooth paste. Press into 9" pie pan and bake at 400 degrees for 15 minutes or until brown and crisp.

One serving counts as:	Fruit	Milk	Bread ◖
Freedom to Choose Calories:	Vegetable	Fat	Protein

VEGGIE PIZZA

Makes 8 servings.

CRUST:

1   8 oz. (8 count) tube refrigerated crescent rolls

Press into bottom of 13" x 9" baking dish. Prick with fork and bake for 8-10 minutes at 350 degrees. Cool.

FILLING:

1 1/3 c. Vegetable Dip (24 oz. carton cottage cheese and 1 pkg. Hidden Valley Ranch Mix combined in blender)

5 Tbsp. & 1 tsp. diet mayonnaise

Mix and spread on cooled crust.

TOPPING:

4 c. fresh vegetables

4 oz. sharp cheddar cheese, shredded

Press any of the following vegetables cut into small pieces onto filling: broccoli, cauliflower, cherry tomato, red or green peppers, green onion, mushrooms, grated carrots, sliced radishes, etc.

Top with cheese. Chill 2 hours or overnight.

One serving counts as:	Fruit		Milk		Bread ●
Freedom to Choose Calories:	Vegetable ●		Fat ●		Protein ◖

CAULIFLOWER CHEESE CASSEROLE

Makes 2 servings.

1   10 oz. pkg. frozen cauliflower or broccoli

Cook cauliflower or broccoli. Drain. Place in 1 quart baking dish coated with nonstick cooking spray.

2 large eggs

2/3 c. cottage cheese

1 Tbsp. minced onion flakes

salt and pepper

Blend eggs, cottage cheese, onion flakes, salt, and pepper in blender until smooth. Pour over cauliflower or broccoli.

Bake 30 minutes uncovered at 350 degrees.

One serving counts as:	Fruit		Milk		Bread
Freedom to Choose Calories:	Vegetable ●●		Fat		Protein ●●

ISLAND CARROT SALAD

Makes 1 serving.

1/2 c. grated carrots
1/2 c. pineapple tidbits canned in their own juice (not drained)
2 tsp. diet mayonnaise
1 tsp. plain, NONfat yogurt
1/2 tsp. coconut extract

Combine all ingredients.

One serving counts as:	Fruit ●	Milk	Bread
Freedom to Choose Calories: **2**	Vegetable ●	Fat ●	Protein

CUCUMBER SALAD

Makes 10 servings.

4 c. cucumbers, peeled and thinly sliced
1 c. thin onion rings

Mix cucumbers and onion.

1/2 c. vinegar
1/2 c. water
1/4 tsp. salt
dash pepper
6 pkts. Equal

Combine vinegar, water, salt, pepper, and sweetener. Mix well; pour over onion and cucumbers.

Chill until cucumbers are wilted. Garnish with dill or parsley.

One serving counts as:	Fruit	Milk	Bread
Freedom to Choose Calories:	Vegetable ●	Fat	Protein

TOMATO MOZZARELLA SALAD

Makes 4 servings.

2 large tomatoes, sliced (2 cups)
4 oz. mozzarella cheese, sliced thin

In shallow dish, arrange alternating slices of cheese and tomato.

2 tsp. dried basil
2 tsp. dried oregano
2 Tbsp. finely chopped onion

Sprinkle with spices and onion.

1 Tbsp. & 1 tsp. vegetable oil
1 Tbsp. & 1 tsp. wine vinegar

Drizzle oil and vinegar over top. Serve right away or refrigerate.

One serving counts as:	Fruit	Milk	Bread
Freedom to Choose Calories:	Vegetable ●	Fat ●	Protein ●

CRANBERRY SALAD

Makes 6 servings.

3 c. fresh cranberries (grind after measuring)
1 eight-serving pkg. cherry sugar-free gelatin
1/2 c. boiling water
1 ground apple (not peeled)
1 ground orange (not peeled)
2 c. canned crushed pineapple
6 tsp. sunflower seeds
sugar substitute (use Equal not Sweet N Low) to taste

Dissolve gelatin in boiling water. Cool slightly and add rest of ingredients as indicated.

One serving counts as:	Fruit ●◖	Milk	Bread
Freedom to Choose Calories: **31**	Vegetable	Fat	Protein

ZERO SALAD DRESSING

Makes 1 serving.

1/2 c. tomato juice
1 Tbsp. lemon juice or vinegar
1 Tbsp. finely chopped onion

Pepper and other spices, as well as chopped parsley or green pepper, may be added if desired. Sugar substitute may be added if desired.

Combine ingredients in a jar with tightly fitted top. Shake well. Store in refrigerator.

One serving counts as:	Fruit	Milk	Bread
Freedom to Choose Calories:	Vegetable ●	Fat	Protein

PICKLED BEETS

Makes 4 servings.

1 16 oz. can sliced beets, undrained
1 1/3 c. cider vinegar
1/2 c. sliced onion
1 Tbsp. mixed pickling spice
salt and pepper to taste

Combine all ingredients in saucepan and heat to boiling. Cool to room temperature. Chill, covered, several hours before serving. If some sweetness is desired, add some artificial sweetener.

One serving counts as:	Fruit	Milk	Bread
Freedom to Choose Calories:	Vegetable ●◗	Fat	Protein

MIXED GREEN SALAD WITH BUTTERMILK DRESSING

Makes 4 servings.

4 c. chilled Boston lettuce leaves
3 c. chilled spinach leaves, washed well
1 large egg, hard-cooked and chopped
Buttermilk Dressing (see below)

BUTTERMILK DRESSING:
1 Tbsp. plus 1 tsp. mayonnaise
1 Tbsp. white vinegar, heated
2 tsp. Dijon-style mustard
1/2 c. buttermilk
1/2 tsp. Worcestershire sauce
dash white pepper

Tear leaves into bite-size pieces. In large salad bowl combine lettuce and spinach; add Buttermilk Dressing (below) and toss to coat.

Sprinkle with chopped egg and serve immediately.

In small bowl combine mayonnaise, vinegar, and mustard, mixing well; gradually beat in milk and seasonings.

One serving counts as:	Fruit	Milk	Bread
Freedom to Choose Calories: **15**	Vegetable ●●●◖	Fat ●	Protein ◤

CREAMED MUSHROOM SAUCE

Makes 2 servings.

1 c. sliced mushrooms (packed tight)
1 pkt. chicken broth & seasoning mix
1/4 c. water
2 Tbsp. instant nonfat dry milk

Cut firm white mushrooms lengthwise, so that each has some cap and stem. Put in nonstick saucepan with broth mix and water. Cover and cook 5 minutes. Stir in milk and turn off heat. Excellent over chicken, fish, or vegetables.

One serving counts as:	Fruit	Milk	Bread
Freedom to Choose Calories: **35**	Vegetable ●	Fat	Protein

STUFFED PEPPERS

Makes 2 servings.

1/2 lb. ground turkey
1/2 c. chopped onion

Brown turkey and onion; drain.

salt and pepper to taste
1 tsp. chili powder
1 Tbsp. Worcestershire sauce
1 tsp. prepared mustard
1/2 c. tomato juice
1 c. cooked rice OR macaroni
2 whole green peppers, cleaned and cored

Add salt, pepper, chili powder, Worcestershire sauce, mustard, tomato juice, and cooked rice OR macaroni. Mix well and put into green peppers.

Bake at 350 degrees for 45 minutes.

One serving counts as:	Fruit	Milk	Bread ●
Freedom to Choose Calories:	Vegetable ● ● ●	Fat	Protein ● ● ●

SAUERKRAUT SALAD

Makes 12 servings.

1 qt. (4 c.) sauerkraut, drained

Put sauerkraut in strainer, run cold water through it, and drain well.

1/2 c. vinegar
18-24 pkts. Equal
1/4 c. salad oil

Combine vinegar, Equal, and oil.

1/2 c. onion, chopped
1/2 c. green pepper, cut fine
1 1/2 c. celery, diced
1 small jar pimento, cut fine

Add to vegetables and mix with sauerkraut. Let stand overnight in refrigerator.

One serving counts as:	Fruit	Milk	Bread
Freedom to Choose Calories:	Vegetable ●	Fat ●	Protein

CRANBERRY SAUCE

Makes 4 servings.

1 1/2 c. low calorie cranberry juice, divided
1/2 c. fresh or frozen cranberries—no sugar

In small saucepan combine 1 1/4 cups cranberry juice with the cranberries, and over high heat, bring to a boil. Cook, stirring occasionally, until liquid reduces and berries split, about 5 minutes.

2 tsp. cornstarch
1 Tbsp. granulated sugar
Garnish: shredded orange peel

Add cornstarch and sugar to remaining 1/4 cup juice, stirring until cornstarch is dissolved; pour mixture into saucepan and, stirring constantly, allow mixture to return to a full boil. Reduce heat to low and cook for 1 minute longer. Serve hot or chilled, garnished with orange peel.

One serving counts as:	Fruit ◖	Milk	Bread
Freedom to Choose Calories: **20**	Vegetable	Fat	Protein

CREAM OF TOMATO SOUP

Makes 1 serving.

1 c. (8 oz.) tomato juice
1 bouillon cube
2/3 c. cottage cheese

Combine in blender. Pour into saucepan and warm until heated through.

One serving counts as:	Fruit	Milk	Bread
Freedom to Choose Calories: **10**	Vegetable ●●	Fat	Protein ●●

TWELVE LAYER SALAD

Makes 8 servings.

6   four-serving size pkgs. sugar-free gelatin: cherry, lime, lemon, orange, raspberry, and strawberry
2 c. plain, lowfat yogurt

Add 1 c. boiling water to cherry gelatin; take out half and very slowly add 1/3 c. yogurt. Pour into 9 x 13" glass pan. Chill 20 minutes or until firm. Add 3 Tbsp. cold water to remaining half of gelatin and pour carefully on top of first layer. Repeat with each flavor.

One serving counts as:	Fruit	Milk ◖	Bread
Freedom to Choose Calories: **24**	Vegetable	Fat	Protein

HARVARD BEETS

Makes 4 servings.

2   16 oz. cans whole baby beets (4 cups)

Drain liquid into measuring cup and add water if necessary, to make 1 cup.

To liquid add:
1/4 c. vinegar
4 tsp. sugar
4 pkts. Sweet N Low
4 tsp. cornstarch
dash EACH cinnamon, nutmeg, and mace

Cook sauce over medium heat until thickened and translucent. Add beets and cook until just heated through. Divide beets and sauce equally.

One serving counts as:	Fruit	Milk	Bread
Freedom to Choose Calories: **30**	Vegetable ● ●	Fat	Protein

GRAVY

Makes 1 serving.

1/2 tsp. instant beef bouillon
1/2 tsp. Worcestershire sauce
1/4 c. water
1/4 c. skim milk

Boil first four ingredients together, then remove from heat.

1 tsp. margarine
2 tsp. flour

In another pan mix margarine and flour over a medium heat until a ball forms. Cook an additional minute, being careful not to let mixture burn. Reduce heat and carefully pour liquid mixture into the pan with the flour mixture. Using a wire whip, stir constantly until all of the flour mixture is dissolved. Increase heat, bringing to a boil, until the gravy thickens.

One serving counts as:	Fruit	Milk ◣	Bread
Freedom to Choose Calories: **25**	Vegetable	Fat ●	Protein

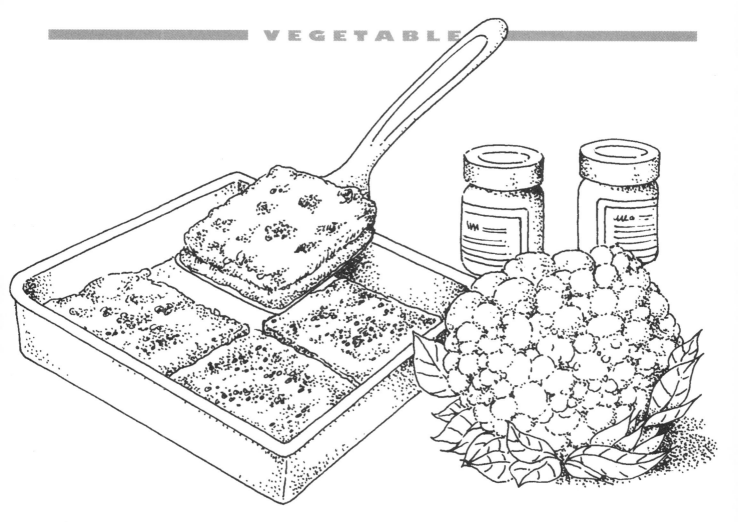

VEGETABLE WITH CHEESE AU GRATIN TOPPING

Makes 1 serving.

1 1/2 c. cooked vegetable (asparagus, green beans, broccoli, cabbage, cauliflower, eggplant, etc.)
1/2 c. fresh or canned mushrooms, drained and sliced
2 oz. hard cheese, grated
1/2 tsp. mixed dried herbs (parsley, chives, basil, etc.)
salt and pepper

In small casserole layer vegetable, mushrooms, cheese (reserve 2 Tbsp.), and herbs; sprinkle with salt and pepper.

1/4 c. tomato juice
1 slice bread (not diet), made into crumbs

Stir in tomato juice. Mix reserved cheese with bread crumbs and spread on top of vegetable.

Bake at 350 degrees until hot and bubbly.

One serving counts as:	Fruit	Milk	Bread ●
Freedom to Choose Calories:	Vegetable ●●●●●◖	Fat	Protein ●●

LIVER CHOP SUEY

Makes 2 servings.

8 oz. liver, cubed
1/2 c. water
1 beef bouillon cube
2 pkts. Sweet N Low
2 Tbsp. soy sauce
2 Tbsp. dry onion flakes

Brown liver in nonstick pan. Add water, bouillon, Sweet N Low, soy sauce, and onion flakes. Cover and simmer 15 minutes.

1 c. diced celery
2 c. shredded cabbage
1 c. cooked rice

Add celery; cook 5 minutes. Add cabbage, cook until cabbage is tender. Serve on a bed of rice.

One serving counts as:		Fruit	Milk	Bread ●
Freedom to Choose Calories: **10**		Vegetable ●●●	Fat	Protein ●●●

BRAISED LIVER CREOLE

Makes 2 servings.

12 oz. beef liver
3/4 c. beef broth

Cook liver in beef broth in nonstick skillet over moderate heat 5 minutes or until liver is lightly browned.

1/4 tsp. onion salt
1/8 tsp. pepper
1/2 c. coarsley chopped onions
1/2 c. tomato puree
1/2 c. water
1/2 c. coarsley chopped green pepper
1 c. sliced celery
2 Tbsp. chili powder

Sprinkle with onion salt and pepper. Add onion, tomato puree, water, green pepper, celery, and chili powder. Cook covered over low heat 15 minutes or until liver is cooked throughout.

One serving counts as:		Fruit	Milk	Bread
Freedom to Choose Calories: **15**		Vegetable ●●◖	Fat	Protein ●●●◖

CALVES LIVER WITH GRAPES

Makes 2 servings.

8 oz. sliced calves liver

Using a knife or kitchen scissors, cut liver into 1" strips.

salt and pepper

Season lightly with salt and pepper. Cook quickly in nonstick skillet. As soon as strips are brown on all sides, divide equally onto 2 serving plates; keep hot.

2 tsp. lemon juice
24 large or 40 small seedless green grapes
2 tsp. margarine

Pour lemon juice and grapes into skillet and mash a few of the grapes to release their juices. Heat quickly; remove from heat and divide evenly over liver strips. Stir 1 tsp. margarine into each serving.

2 tsp. minced parsley

Garnish with parsley.

| *One serving counts as:* | Fruit ● | Milk | Bread |
| Freedom to Choose Calories: | Vegetable | Fat ● | Protein ● ● ● |

BOILED LIVER

Boil liver by dropping strips or slices into boiling salted water. Cook briefly at a fast simmer until just done; don't overcook it.

Weigh cooked portion.

BROILED LIVER

Makes 1 serving.

4 oz. sliced liver
1 tsp. margarine
lemon juice
watercress (opt.)

Broil liver quickly (1-2 minutes per side) about 3" from heat. Spread with a teaspoon of margarine, and sprinkle with lemon juice and minced watercress before serving.

| *One serving counts as:* | Fruit | Milk | Bread |
| Freedom to Choose Calories: | Vegetable | Fat ● | Protein ● ● ● |

LIVER BURGER

Makes 2 servings.

10 oz. beef liver
2 tsp. lemon juice
salt and pepper to taste

Season liver with lemon juice, salt, and pepper. Broil until thoroughly cooked.

toasted dehydrated onion flakes
1/2 c. canned drained mushrooms, chopped

Combine onion flakes with mushrooms.

4 slices diet bread
4 tsp. diet mayonnaise
1 tsp. prepared mustard
1/2 c. sliced tomato
1/4 c. dill pickle, sliced
1/2 c. shredded lettuce

Toast bread. Spread with mayonnaise, mustard, and shredded lettuce. Cover with onion flakes, mushrooms, liver, tomato slices, and pickle. Top with another slice of bread.

One serving counts as:		Fruit	Milk	Bread ●
Freedom to Choose Calories:		Vegetable ●◖	Fat ●	Protein ●●●●

BAKED LIVER

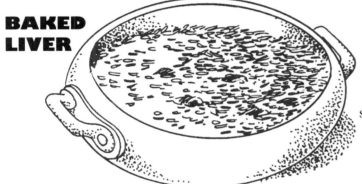

Bake whole liver at 350 degrees until it is tender, 45-50 minutes. Weigh portions, and serve still juicy. For a meal-in-one oven dish, surround liver with vegetables such as sliced onions, carrots, tomatoes, green pepper, and even sliced potatoes—all in allowed amounts. Whole liver may also be cooked in a large covered skillet on top of range.

PANBROILED LIVER

Makes 1 serving.

4 oz. beef or veal liver

Pan broil sliced liver in a nonstick or heavy skillet coated with nonstick cooking spray, until done on both sides, but still pink inside, about 4-5 minutes. Remove liver from pan.

1/4 c. green pepper, diced
1/2 c. onion, diced
1/4 c. celery, diced
1 beef bouillon cube

Cook vegetables in the skillet with a little water and bouillon cube until they are almost tender and liquid is mostly evaporated. Add slices of liver, cover pan, and steam, turning liver once.

One serving counts as:		Fruit	Milk	Bread
Freedom to Choose Calories: 10		Vegetable ●●	Fat	Protein ●●●

MARINATED LIVER

TO MARINATE LIVER—Cover with chicken bouillon or with dietetic ginger ale and let stand 30 minutes. Drain and cook.

LIVER MONTE CARLO

Makes 1 serving.

6 oz. calf, beef, or chicken liver
2 tsp. tomato juice

Pour tomato juice over liver in a shallow baking dish.

1/8 tsp. garlic powder
1/4 tsp. fennel seeds
salt and pepper to taste

Sprinkle remaining ingredients on top. Broil about 4" from heat until desired doneness.

One serving counts as:	Fruit	Milk	Bread
Freedom to Choose Calories:	Vegetable	Fat	Protein ●●●●

LIVER SWEET AND SOUR

Makes 2 servings.

1/2 c. pineapple
1 c. tomato juice
1 Tbsp. vinegar
1/2 Tbsp. soy sauce
brown sugar substitute to equal 1 Tbsp. brown sugar
1/2 tsp. instant beef bouillon

Drain pineapple and save juice. Add water to juice to make 1/4 cup; add tomato juice, vinegar, soy sauce, brown sugar substitute, and bouillon. Bring to a boil.

8 oz. liver

Cut liver into 1" strips and add to hot liquid mixture. Cover and simmer 15 minutes.

2 tsp. cornstarch
2 Tbsp. water

Combine cornstarch with 2 Tbsp. water and stir into hot mixture; stir until thick.

1/2 c. green pepper, chopped
1/4 c. onion, chopped

Add pepper, onion, and pineapple. Simmer 7 minutes.

One serving counts as:	Fruit ◖	Milk	Bread
Freedom to Choose Calories: 15	Vegetable ●◖	Fat	Protein ●●●

INDEX

A

9" Pie Crust 69
Almost a Pie 11
Apple Peanut Butter Dream 37
Apple Raisin Brown Betty 44
Apple Spiced Oatmeal 15
Apricot Dreams 43
Asparagus Tuna Bake 34

B

Baked Banana 39
Baked Frittata 27
Baked Haddock with Mountain Yogurt Sauce 33
Baked Liver 81
Baked Squash 11
Banana Fluff Pudding 23
Banana Split Breakfast 45
Banana Split Pie 41
Blueberry Crumble 40
Blueberry Freeze 45
Blueberry Pancakes 19
Boiled Liver 80
Braised Liver Creole 79
Bread Pudding 15
Breakfast Bar 16
Breakfast "Taco" 24
Broiled Liver 80
Brownies 13
Buttery Milk 57

C

Cabbage Meal in One 48
Calves Liver with Grapes 80
Carrot and Pineapple Mold 65
Cauliflower Cheese Casserole 70
Cheese and Potato Ragout 67
Cheese Souffle 25
Chicken Chow Mein 50
Chili Beef Dinner 50
Chocolate Applesauce Cupcakes 19
Chocolate Cream Soda 60
Chocolate Peanut Butter Slurpie 59
Cinnamon Apple Bread Pudding 21
Coconut Bread Pudding 29
Coconut Macaroon Cookies 63
Cranberry Gelee 38
Cranberry Salad 72
Cranberry Sauce 75

Cream of Tomato Soup 75
Creamed Mushroom Sauce 73
Creamed Tuna 31
Creamy Carrot Soup 67
Crustless Asparagus Quiche 28
Cucumber Salad 71

D-E

Deviled Eggs 22
Egg Foo Yung 22
Eggless Nog 57
Eggs Au Gratin 26
Eggs Piperade 27

F

Fish Cheeseburger 33
Fowl Cheese 47
French Toast 21
Frozen Fudge Bars 58
Fruit Danish Delight 11
Fruit Ice Cream 55
Fruited Cottage Cheese Mold 42
Fudgesicle 59

G

Gingerbread 18
Grapefruit Meringue 40
Gravy 76
Green Bean Casserole 68
Grilled Flounder Fillets 35

H-I

Happy Pineapple Shake 60
Harvard Beets 76
Hawaiian Beachcomber's Salad 35
Herb-Spinach-Cheese Pie 69
Ice Cream Sandwich 58
Island Carrot Salad 71

L

Layer Salad 65
Legal Fudge 62
Lemon Ice Cream 56
Liver Burger 81
Liver Chop Suey 79

Liver Monte Carlo 82
Liver Sweet and Sour 82

M-N

Macaroni Cheese Bake 13
Marinated Liver 82
Mashed Potato Surprise 16
Meatballs 52
Milk Froth 55
Milk Sherbet 57
Milky Fudge Bars 61
Mixed Green Salad with Buttermilk Dressing 73
Molded Cranberry Waldorf Salad 38
Mountain Yogurt Sauce 33
Mushroom Asparagus Omelet 25
New England Fish Chowder 31

O-P

Oat Bran Muffins 17
Orange Milk Freeze 62
Panbroiled Liver 81
Peach Cobbler 43
Peach Crisp 44
Peach Nectar 56
Pepper Mates 48
Pickled Beets 72
Pina Colada 56
Pineapple Upside-down Custard 24
Pizza Casserole 49
Pizza Treat 17
Pleasing Pumpkin Pie 12
Poached Eggs and Broccoli 28
Potato Charlies 18
Pumpkin Dessert 16
Pumpkin Pudding 12

R

Really Good Goulash 49
Refrigerator Apple Butter 42
Rhubarb Pie 14
Rice Like Pudding 61

S

Salmon Delight 34
Salmon Loaf 32
Sauerkraut Salad 74
Second Time Turkey 52
Sloppy Joes 53
Snow Eggs 26
Stir Fry Chicken and Vegetables 51
Stir Fry Vegetables 68
Strawberry Cheese Bavarian 37
Strawberry Cheesecake 41
Strawberry Ice Cream 55
Strawberry Mousse 45
Strawberry Puff 40
Strawberry Yogurt Frost 58
Stuffed Peppers 74
Summer Slaw 68
Sunshine Orange Cake 63
Sweet Fruit 'N' Noodle Pudding 39

T-U

Tacos 53
Tasty Cod 32
Tofu Shake 42
Tomato Mozzarella Salad 71
Tomato Soup 67
Tuna Stuffed Tomato 31
Twelve Layer Salad 75
Unbelievable Lasagna 47

V-W

Vanilla Shake 60
Vegetable with Cheese Au Gratin Topping 77
Veggie Pizza 70
Weigh to Win Snicker Bars 62
Whipped Cauliflower 66
Whole Wheat Muffins 14

Y-Z

Yogurt Cucumber Salad 66
Yogurt Egg Salad 29
Yogurt Whip 59
Zero Salad Dressing 72
Zucchini Omelet 23